A MOST PERNICIOUS THING

Gun Trading and Native Warfare in the Early Contact Period

BRIAN J. GIVEN

A MOST PERNICIOUS THING

Gun Trading and Native Warfare in the Early Contact Period

BRIAN J. GIVEN

Carleton University Press
Ottawa, Canada
1994

Printed and bound in Canada

Canadian Cataloguing in Publication Data

Given, Brian J. (Brian James), 1952–

    A most pernicious thing : gun trading and Native warfare in the early contact period

Includes bibliographical references.
ISBN 0-88629-222-0 (bound).–
   ISBN 0-88629-223-9 (pbk.)

    1. Indian of North American–First Contact with Europeans. 2. Indians of North America–History–Colonial period, ca. 1600–1775. 3. Indians of North America–Foreign influences. 5. Firearms and trade–North America I. Title.

E45.G48 1994   970.004'97   C93–090642–X

Carleton University Press
160 Paterson Hall, 1125 Colonel By Dr.
Ottawa K1S 5B6 Canada
(613)788–3740

Distributed in Canada by:
Oxford University Press Canada
70 Wynford Dr., Don Mills, ON M3C 1J9
(416)441–2941

Cover Design: Aerographics Ottawa
Interior: Campbell Typesetting Winnipeg

Acknowledgements

Carleton University Press gratefully acknowledges the support extended to its publishing programme by the Canada Council and the Ontario Arts Council.

The Press would also like to thank the Department of Communications, Government of Canada, and the Government of Ontario through the Ministry of Culture, Tourism and Recreation, for their assistance.

This book has been published with the help of a grant from the Social Science Federation of Canada, using funds provided by the Social Sciences and Humanities Research Council of Canada.

*To my parents, Jim and Phyllis
and to my wife Heather
and daughter Alexis.*

Contents

Acknowledgments

Chapter One
Contemporary Ethnohistory   **1**

Chapter Two
The Gun in Europe - Evolution and Deployment   **13**

Chapter Three
Colonial Arms   **33**

Chapter Four
The Native/European Gun Trade Before 1640   **49**

Chapter Five
The Weapons Trade Begins in Earnest   **57**

Chapter Six
1655 to the End of King Philip's War 1676   **81**

Chapter Seven
The Musket - Operational Parameters   **93**

Chapter Eight
Conclusions and Hypotheses   **111**

Appendix
Notes on Lethality   **119**

Bibliography   **121**

Illustrations
1. Sketch of a matchlock   **16**
2. Sketch of a flintlock   **29**
3. Detail from Samuel de Champlain's sketch   **37**

Acknowledgments

Much of the research for this book was done for a Master's thesis supervised by Professor Bruce Cox. I thank him for his help then and more recently, as my friend and colleague at Carleton, for his encouragement and comments on the manuscript. I owe much to the librarians and staff of the University of Illinois Library at Champagne-Urbana, the Newberry Library in Chicago, the New York State Archives at Albany, the Canadian National Archives and the Canadian National Archives Library in Ottawa. I especially want to express my appreciation to the most helpful and knowledgeable librarians at Interlibrary Loans, Carleton University. The staff at the War Museum of Canada were always helpful and I especially want to thank Mr. John Chown for his generosity. Pam Mitchell typed the original manuscript and made numerous corrections with speed and accuracy. The sketches of lock designs on pages sixteen and twenty-nine are the work of our friend Edwina Billyk. My editor, Jennifer Strickland of Carleton University Press, patiently pointed out several times that I wasn't done yet.

Their help and scholarship have contributed to the merit of this work, and its flaws are no one's responsibility but my own.

Chapter One

Contemporary Ethnohistory

Civilization in the Americas may be as old as forty thousand years and is certainly not younger than twenty thousand. The first immigrants journeyed across the Bering Strait land bridge from Siberia during the Pleistocene era and it is clear that they had occupied the length and breadth of the continent by about seventeen thousand years ago. There is much dispute about the size of the population of what Europeans ironically called the New World when they discovered it at the end of the fifteenth century. Estimates range from as few as 8.4 million to a high estimate of 112 million persons.[1] When the Europeans arrived, less than four hundred years ago, this was a populated continent. Yet the French, English, Spanish and, to a lesser extent, the Swedish and Dutch newcomers so successfully displaced or eliminated the original residents of the Americas that our present civilization is almost entirely Euro-centric. For many of us, the history of the continent begins in 1492.

Our conception of the New World as virgin territory has been reinforced by our continued practice of referring to millions of members of about two thousand ancient cultures, speaking in as many different languages, as "Indians." We do this because a confused Christopher Columbus was under the impression that the Caribbean island of Hispaniola was the West Indies.

This image of the New World as empty, waiting to be filled in satisfaction of European markets, conflicts and dreams is linked to

---

[1] This figure is based on the argument that new diseases killed up to eighty million inhabitants of North and South America.

European constructions of its homogeneous inhabitants as "primitive." It is easiest, of course, to rationalize the occupation of a land with *no* inhabitants. That conception was sustainable in a European context and many Europeans believed it to be so. But, faced with the Narragansett, Pequot, Iroquois, Wampanoag, Huron and dozens of other cultures, the early colonists were unable to maintain it. If the Natives were irrefutably *there*, one possible response was to see them as not *really* there, as nomadic and, by implication, as living nowhere. This worked for the Algonkian-speaking peoples who lived north of the Huron but could hardly describe tribes like the Huron with their vast cornfields, extensive trade networks and permanent villages. The only alternative was the rationale that the inhabitants of the New World were empty *themselves*, of culture and perhaps even of the potential for culture. It was necessary for the advancement of civilization that they be dominated: it might even do them good. The development of this rationale was encouraged by warfare, accompanied as always by the necessity to dehumanize the enemy.

In reality, virtually all of the land in North America was occupied when the European colonists arrived. While there was accommodation on both sides, conflict was inevitable (for example, Virginia 1622, the Pequot War 1636–37, King Philip's War of 1675–76) and armed confrontation ranging from minor skirmishes to full-scale warfare continued for more than 150 years.

The earliest European descriptions of aboriginal North Americans characterize them as civilized people, physically attractive, strong and dignified in their bearing and of mental acuity on a par with their European guests. During the period of conquest, resistance and displacement, a new characterization of Natives as physically primal, limited in cultural potential and intellectually inferior, surfaced. Such a characterization was part of what Jennings (1975) has called the "Cant of Conquest."

Anthropological portrayals of Native North Americans have invariably both guided and reflected demands of the colonial and the post-colonial enterprises. First of all, Native history is acknowledged mainly as a counterpoint to that of Europeans in North America. Before the Europeans arrived Natives had *pre*-history. We constructed for them a separate category of race[2] and decades of research was dedicated to identifying their racial characteristics.[3]

---

[2] Carolus Linnaeus created the category of the "American" or "Red" race in 1735.
[3] Of course no constellation of traits was discovered which sufficiently distinguished Native Americans to justify the use of the concept of race.

As our discipline and our culture began to abandon the notion that populations could be ranked or even distinguished with reference to a phylogenetic taxonomy[4] we embraced a new, more egalitarian notion. While the "other" was not characterized by what Lubbock called "extreme mental inferiority,"[5] he/she was enculturated within a "primitive society." They were still inferior but it was not their fault and they could learn to be civilized like Europeans, at least if they started as children. This was the rationale behind a vast array of assimilationist interventions ranging from the banning of the northwest-coast potlatch to Canada's barbaric residential-schools policies, which were in place as late as the 1960s. It is noteworthy that this conception, while preferable to the assumption of racial inferiority, justified the negation of the right of Native adults to self-determination.

Beginning in the ethnographies of the 1920s and echoing throughout the anthropology of this century, the concept of "cultural relativity" reached its present zenith in recent postmodern critiques (for example, Clifford and Marcus 1986). This relativist perspective increasingly informs our contemporary ethnographic research and theory and is beginning to inform popular attitudes toward contemporary Native peoples. Recent public questioning of the symbolic statements inherent in Columbus Day celebrations in the United States is some indication that North Americans are willing to question what they have been taught about how North America came to be occupied almost entirely by Europeans. This is important because conceptions of our own culture and of the cultures of others derive much of their authority from what we believe about our and their history. The writing of history has consequences for the future.

Within recent memory, a minister of the government of Canada implied, during a discussion of aboriginal rights, that when Europeans encountered the Indians the latter were so primitive that they had not invented the wheel: "Why, when we came here, they were still dragging things around on two sticks."[6] While many were horrified by this remark, which appeared to reflect a profound contempt for Native culture, then

---

[4] This is a task which is properly begun but hardly completed.

[5] Lubbock states that advanced ideas are "entirely beyond the mental range of the lower savages whose extreme mental inferiority we have much difficulty in realizing." (Lubbock 1870:5)

[6] Then Defence Minister James Richardson is reported to have said (in 1975) of Canadian Indians: "What did they ever do for Canada? Did they discover oil? They didn't even invent the wheel. Why, when we came here, they were still dragging things around on two sticks!" Quoted in an article by columnist Roy MacGregor, *The Ottawa Citizen*, August 23, 1988, p. A-3.

and now, it cannot be denied that the assumptions upon which it was based are widespread. Many non-Native North Americans believe that the Native peoples were "primitive" when they first encountered the "civilized" Europeans during the seventeenth century. Given our culture's portrayal of Indians in popular (and, too often, in scholarly) literature and in the media, it is hardly surprising that many non-Native North Americans react to claims for aboriginal rights by suggesting that, whatever their present situation, Indians are better off now than they would be had they remained "in the stone age." After all, were not the Indians' ancestors more than anxious to give up the tools and techniques that characterized their own cultures in order to adopt the ways of the European? Almost from the moment of first contact, didn't the Indians compete desperately with one another for trade with the newcomers, whose material culture was clearly superior to their own?

Anthropologists certainly challenge the characterization of non-literate peoples as "primitive." We are not, however, entirely immune from our culture's assumption that our ancestors were more sophisticated or advanced than the predecessors of contemporary Native Canadians. While we disagree about the nature of the connection between technology and culture, we are in almost universal agreement that the Europeans who settled in North America during the seventeenth century brought with them inventories of material culture which the aboriginal peoples were anxious to acquire and on which they rapidly became dependent, eventually losing the ability to survive, or at least the willingness to survive, without the products of European culture. This is the concept of "trade-dependence." The notion that trade-dependence rapidly developed among Native peoples in contact with Europeans serves as a conceptual licence for the acceptance of our European informants' valuations, or rather de-valuations, of other aspects of seventeenth century Native culture.

Clearly, such a view of Native history has an impact which is not limited to the academic concerns of the ethnohistorian but which is also relevant to contemporary issues such as aboriginal-rights claims. These claims are based on the Native Canadian belief that European hegemony in North America has been very much to their detriment. Perhaps even more importantly, the incorrect but common assumption that Native North American culture was unable to compete with that of the Europeans for the hearts and minds of its own members challenges the dignity and sense of self-worth of contemporary Indians.

It is therefore very important that we understand the relationship between our analyses of contemporary cultures and our analyses of their history. In this chapter I will briefly discuss issues relating to cross-cultural historical reconstruction and will argue that a detailed re-examination of our assumptions regarding early Native Canadian ethnohistory is in order. Because firearms are the commonly cited locus for early trade-dependence, Chapters Two to Seven examine the trade in firearms to Native peoples as a case study. I will challenge the notion that Native peoples believed this technology to be superior to their own or that they became in any way dependent on it and consequently on the colonists. Toward this end I will discuss at some length the European development of hand-held firearms, including operational parameters such as accuracy and rate of fire. I will also demonstrate that Native weapons technology was superior to available firearms, and consequently that Native acquisition of these goods must be understood with reference to their symbolic rather than pragmatic value. Chapter Eight addresses general issues of ethnohistorical reconstruction and offers explanations for the dissonance between the likely historical reality discussed as a case study in earlier chapters and traditional ethnohistorical and popular treatments.

Cross-Cultural Historical Reconstruction

I suggested above that our valuation and understanding of the cultures of contemporary peoples is predicated to some extent upon our understanding of their history and cultural heritage. In other words, social anthropology is never entirely separate from ethnohistorical beliefs. At best, these beliefs reflect contemporary ethnohistorical theories regarding the cultural heritage of the people in question. At worst, the contemporary social anthropologist has, as a starting point for research, myths about the subject group that may be more informative about the historical needs of the anthropologist's culture than about the people in question. Historical reconstructions invariably reflect the concerns and assumptions of a particular generation of scholars. No historical analysis is unbiased. Hence any historical account is both a chronicle of events past and a reflection of contemporary issues. No historian would make the mistake of reading a historical account as if it were solely about the past. To make matters even more confusing, the information on which historians must draw in order to create their analyses can never be an objective or complete account of a sequence of events. Our long-dead informants were individuals who can only have been in one place at one time. For example, accounts of events written by men may underrepresent or ignore altogether the experiences of women, while members of one social class are unlikely to know about or to understand the actions of another. Similarly, accounts of interactions between cultures, when written by members of only one of the cultures, invariably give expression to the concerns of the informants' group and de-emphasize or distort those of the other. We must also remember that only recently have we recognized the need to attempt to understand inter-cultural events from a cultural perspective other than our own.

One of anthropology's major contributions to western culture has been the concept of "cultural relativity," the notion that the norms, values and actions that characterize a given culture cannot be understood, and therefore must not be judged, within the frame of reference constituted by the norms and values of another. Contemporary anthropologists strive to avoid such ethnocentric portrayals while recognizing that "objectivity" is a myth of modernism. Instead, we attempt to construct ethnographies that take into account the unique histories, ecologies, social, political and economic environments that have shaped the societies we study. We recognize that, just as to understand the personality of an adult we must know about the individual's life history, so to understand a contemporary culture we must know what collective experiences it encodes. This means that modern ethnographers seek to construct models that reflect the experiences and world view of the members of the cultures studied. Modern historians recognize that accounts of cross-cultural interactions require reconstructions of the perspectives of all parties.

When we reconstruct a historical account of a sequence of events involving two or more literate cultures, we are faced with the daunting prospect of reconstructing two or more ways of seeing a sequence of events, and then of reconstructing the events themselves in light of the concerns that characterize our own contemporary scholarship. At the same time, we must recognize that we are introducing concepts and interpretations that may not reflect the subjective experience of our informants. These problems of reconstruction are magnified incalculably when our sole source of information about past cross-cultural interactions consists in accounts written from one point of view. Unfortunately, this is usually the case when we investigate past interactions between a literate and a non-literate culture.

This latter difficulty is compounded when the societies in question were in conflict and when we are especially interested in understanding the attitudes and actions of the vanquished. The victors in any conflict are always able, to some extent, to write history as a rationalization of their own actions. Where the vanquished society is non-literate, contrary information is minimized. A non-literate, subjugated people may be historically recreated by the victors in ways that are consistent with the latter's need to justify their past and present actions.

All of these difficulties are embodied in our attempts to understand the early period of Native/European contact in North America. The European settlers of the seventeenth century left a variety of written records that enable us to construct a complex picture of life in the colonies. They also provide us with the colonists' observations and opinions regarding the lives of Native peoples, especially with regard to their interactions with the Europeans. This is, of course, a one-sided view and nowhere is it more suspect than when it relates to potential or actual armed confrontation between Natives and Whites. Yet the perspective of our colonial informants tends to be incorporated relatively uncritically into our ethnohistory of the period.

Upon this shaky foundation, ethnohistorical edifices have been constructed which are both historically inaccurate and demeaning to the sophistication and integrity of traditional Native societies. These reconstructions of events during the course of Native/European early contact profoundly influence our contemporary attitudes toward Native people. It is incumbent on the ethnohistorian to constantly re-evaluate the use of archival material, especially when that material is so clearly biased. The bases for the application of such powerful concepts as trade-dependence must be re-examined through highly specific case studies. As such a case study, I will examine, in the following chapters, the application of the notion of "trade-dependence" to Native warfare during the "Iroquois Wars" of the mid-1600s. This case study is significant for three reasons. Firstly, the Iroquois Wars culminated in the destruction of the vast Huron Nation by 1655 and thus marked the first massive dispersal of a Native population attributable to the activities of Europeans in North America. Secondly, our European informants, while recognizing that they themselves played a role, blamed the Natives' penchant for war and conquest for this massive disaster. Blaming the victim is a colonialist convention and it seems reasonable to explore the possibility that such an analysis may have been self-serving. Finally, the widely accepted theory I shall challenge argues that dependence on the Europeans' trade in guns caused the Five-Nations[7] to embark on a war of conquest, and further, that the possession of guns made the Five-Nations' victories possible. As the firearm and related paraphernalia are the items most commonly cited as the basis for trade-dependence during the early contact period as well as much later, the trade-gun seems a good place to begin what must become a detailed re-examination of our theories regarding Native trade-dependence.

---

[7] I will use the label "Five-Nations" in place of "Iroquois" because the label is more accurate and is preferred by members of the Five Nations tribes.

The Five-Nations Wars and Native Dependence on European Firearms: A Case Study

Hunt's Hypothesis

Between 1648 and 1652 the Five-Nations, or Iroquois, succeeded in dispersing their traditional enemies, by waging war on an apparently unprecedented scale. Most authors have sought their explanation of these events in the socioeconomic impact of the White man's trade. Specifically, these authors suggest that many Native groups, including the Five-Nations, rapidly became so dependent on European trade that it "instantly divided the tribes into highly competitive groups [such that by 1640 this] trade had become a social and economic necessity to them, their position [having] life or death as alternatives." (Hunt 1972:18)

If such changes occurred they would naturally have given rise to alterations in the pattern and scale of Native alliance and warfare. George Hunt's classic *Wars of the Iroquois* is an example of this line of thought. Hunt advances an economic theory to explain the events that culminated in the destruction or dispersal of a number of tribes, including the Huron, Neutrals, Petun and Ottawas after 1648 (Hunt 1972). Hunt argues that the Five-Nations attempted to usurp the Huron position as middlemen between the Europeans and the fur-producing tribes to the north-west. The Five-Nations felt that this drastic, large-scale action was necessitated by the depletion of their own beaver population from the intensive over-hunting that resulted from their desperation to acquire guns from the Europeans.

Much contemporary scholarship is based, in part, on Hunt's excellent and much reprinted fifty-year-old treatise. Clearly, however, if we are to posit Native trade-dependency both as our implicit premise and as a motivational variable, as do Hunt and his followers (see Goldstein 1969, Tooker 1963), we must demonstrate that such dependence actually existed during the period under discussion. It is necessary to go beyond vague notions of "trade-complex" to specify individual items and to discover which of these became loci of dependency. Secondly, we must be careful to specify what we mean by the term "dependent." Thus, we need studies that investigate the extent of acquisition, and context of use, of specific types of trade items during given time periods. This work presents the findings of a research project which focused on the trade in firearms prior to what Hunt calls the Wars of the Iroquois.

Hunt and other proponents of the dependency hypothesis most often mention firearms as the major locus of such dependency. The premise that European guns of the seventeenth century were vastly superior to aboriginal projectile weapons is pervasive in the literature. For example, Quimby (1966) is able to state that the balance of power between the Huron and the Five-Nations was maintained until 1642, when the Five-Nations were able to obtain more guns from the Dutch. According to Quimby (1966), Otterbein (1965), Tooker (1963) and others, the Five-Nations thus armed were able to overcome the Huron in large-scale wars. We will discuss Schlesier's (1975) sceptical comments on such wars in Chapter Eight.

In concert with Quimby, Hunt argues that the French preference for sending soldiers to protect Native allies, rather than arming them, led to the defeat of the Huron at the hands of the well-armed Five-Nations. Goldstein, (who incorrectly attributes the position to Hunt [1972:7]), discusses the notion that "the supply of firearms and ammunition afforded by the Dutch provoked passion for conquest and aggrandizement among the Five-Nations." (1969:45) Although Hunt does not in fact agree with this analysis of Five-Nations motivation, he does assume that they required guns and ammunition to maintain their military position and, by implication, presumes the superiority of these weapons over those that the Indians could produce themselves: "The Iroquese, being unprovided with Beaver-skins to be given in exchange for guns, powder, ball, and nets would be starved to death, or at least obliged to leave their county." (Thwaites 1896–1901 quoted in Hunt 1972:35) Hunt also writes: "A tribe whose enemies had weapons which it lacked had few alternatives, and all of them were unpleasant. It inevitably made war upon the competitor." (Hunt 1972:19)

Other theorists make even more explicit assumptions. Goldstein (1969) states that with their introduction in the 1500s, guns and ammunition quickly replaced bows and arrows. He shares this assumption with Louise Kellog (1925). Osgoode (1907) asserts that "the Dutch supply of guns and ammunition explains the triumph of the Five-Nations in warfare," and Otterbein (1965) attributes their victories to changing battle tactics resulting from these advances in weapons technology. Tooker (1963), agreeing with Hunt, describes the transition from traditional Five-Nations/Huron blood feud into a full-scale war. In the course of this "national war," the Five-Nations, who were able to secure more guns than their rivals, gradually gained the upper hand (Tooker 1963:117, 122). Trigger (1976:629) even chides Hunt for his conservatism in suggesting that Five-Nations' weapons superiority may not have been as great as others had supposed. Trigger does, however, disagree with Hunt regarding Iroquois motivation; in his more recent book he suggests that Iroquois attacks on their neighbours may have been motivated more by a desire "to prey upon these groups and expand their hunting territories rather than to usurp the Hurons' role as middlemen." (1985:271)

A logical place to begin an examination of the general question of Native trade-dependence in the seventeenth century would be to ask the question "were the Five-Nations dependent upon European weaponry prior to their 1648–52 conflicts with the Huron?"

It cannot be over-emphasized that item-by-item research and analysis is required in order to define the concept of trade-dependence and to determine its usefulness in reconstructing the actions of North American Natives. An effective challenge to the premise that Natives became dependent on firearms during this early period must cast doubt on the usefulness of this concept for understanding Native peoples' perceptions and motivation.

Methodology

The paucity of information relating specifically to the acquisition and use of muskets by the Five-Nations before the war of 1648–52 leaves us little alternative but to combine a straightforward historical approach with a deductive one. Thus, I will ask firstly, whether the Indians could have obtained the weapons; secondly, whether they actually did so; and thirdly, whether such acquisition would have conferred any military advantage upon them. Addressing these issues involves several sets of questions:

1. What kinds of firearms had been developed by the Europeans by the mid-seventeenth century? With reference to the tactical context in which those firearms evolved, which designs might have conferred an advantage on Native users? By what date would such useful weapons have been available to Europeans in North America? These questions are addressed in Chapter Two.

2. Would the colonists, before the Iroquois wars, have been able to trade large numbers of firearms of a type which Indians would have found useful? Would they have been willing to trade them if they could obtain them? I will take up these questions in Chapters Three, Four and Five.

3. Did the Five-Nations, their allies, or their enemies, acquire a significant number of guns prior to the dispersal of the Huron? What types of guns did they acquire? Is there evidence that these weapons gave them any advantage over their enemies or were perceived by them to confer an

advantage? I will return to these questions in Chapters Four, Five and Six.

4.   Did guns of a type which could have been available to Natives in fact offer concrete advantages over traditional weapons in the tactical context in which they would have been used? In what ways did the operational parameters of the musket differ from those of Native projectile weapons? These issues are explored with reference to historical material in Chapter Two and with reference to the author's field-testing in Chapter Seven.

The next chapter provides a discussion of the kinds of firearms which might have been available to the European colonists throughout the first half of the seventeenth century and suggests which types of firearms would have been most useful to Native people. In order to answer this question it is necessary to summarize the evolution and deployment of the European personal firearm with an emphasis on the relative merits of designs which might have been exported to the colonies.

Chapter Three examines the archival evidence for the existence in the French, English and Dutch colonies of quantities of firearms of a type which might have been traded to Native people. We will ask whether the colonists would have been willing and able to trade large numbers of firearms to the Natives before 1648, and whether such guns would have been useful in Indian-style warfare.

Chapter Four examines the earliest trade in firearms to Native people from the beginning of the seventeenth century until the period with which we are most concerned, beginning about 1640. It is important to establish this historical background because Hunt (1972) and his followers use the premise that a large-scale gun trade had developed at a very early date as a springboard to the assumption that the Five-Nations became dependent on the use of guns before 1644.

Chapter Five focuses on the period between 1640 and 1655 and asks whether the Five-Nations, their allies, or their enemies, prior to the dispersal of the Huron, acquired a significant number of guns and what types of guns they received. This chapter also asks whether there is evidence that these weapons gave them any advantage over their enemies (for example, did muskets replace bows and arrows?).

Chapter Six concerns the period between 1655 and King Philip's War in 1675–76 and examines the evidence concerning the development of trade-dependence based upon the personal firearm.

Chapter Seven addresses the question of whether European firearms of the seventeenth century offered performance advantages over Native weapons. Data from an "experimental archaeology" project (Coles 1973) is presented in a discussion of the operational parameters of the seventeenth century musket in comparison to the bow and arrow.

The eighth and final chapter theorizes the disjunction between prevalent assumptions in the ethnohistorical literature regarding early Native trade-dependence on firearms and the probable historical reality.

When Eustace Boulle learned in 1621 that two vessels from La Rochelle had traded for peltries and "had given to the savages a large supply of firearms, with powder, lead, and match," he railed in outrage against the practice: it was "a most pernicious and mischievous thing thus to arm these infidels, who might on occasion use these weapons against us." (Thwaites 1896–1901:32:147, Biggar 1922–36:5:3) Writing the history of conquest can also be pernicious, absolving (as it tends to do) the past and present, while constructing motifs which become the core of dialogue about the future.

Chapter Two

The Gun in Europe –
Evolution and Deployment

In this chapter I will describe the stages in the development of the hand-held firearm reached before 1675. I will examine the types of firearms which were used throughout the sixteenth and seventeenth centuries in western Europe, and when they were used. As was shown in Chapter One, it is necessary to know just what items the Five Nations might have become dependent on. The reader should be warned that it is necessary to draw upon considerable material from the technical history of the hand-held firearm. This detail is needed if we are to work out how many, and which firearms found their way into the hands of Native North Americans during the 1600s. Such technical detail is even more necessary if we are to speculate about the utility of the firearms for the Five-Nations.

During the period from 1600 to 1675, the hand-held firearm evolved from the clumsy "harquebus" of the early Spanish invasions to the sleek, reliable "true flintlock" which was to dominate military arsenals for over two hundred years. The flintlock was used as recently as the Crimean War, and is still considered a serviceable arm in South Africa and some parts of India and South America (Held 1970). Because we are dealing with a rapid evolution over an approximate period of only seventy-five years, it is necessary to be precise in establishing dates for the introduction and use of different evolutionary stages. Nor can we track this technical development solely from the perspective of the North American gun trade. In order to make sense of our story, we need the European perspective.

The "Handgonne" Appears

It is certain that as early as the fourteenth century the use of cannon and other heavy ordinance was widespread in Europe (Held 1970, Wilkinson 1973). During this century, the science of artillery evolved to become a significant new force in warfare on the continent.

While its heavier predecessors were universally used and much esteemed by the year 1400, the hand-held firearm did not appear until about 1475. The first firearms were merely iron tubes welded shut at one end with a touch-hole drilled through the side at the breech end. This barrel, usually of 0.75 cal or less, and of one to two feet in length, was fixed on the end of a handle, rather like the head of a spear (Wilkinson 1970, Greener 1986). Modern historians refer to this weapon as the "hand cannon."

To fire this firearm, its handle was either planted in the ground or clamped in a man's armpit. Fire was applied to the touch-hole using a hot coal or burning tow. If fired point blank at a massed enemy, the hand cannon was a formidable weapon. It was grossly inaccurate, however, more so because it could not be properly aimed.

While greatly inferior to the longbow or crossbow in range, accuracy, and rate of fire, the gun had economic advantages which increased in importance as feudalism declined. The feudal ruler could maintain a standing army, the members of which could gain proficiency in the use of their weapons, thus taking advantage of the longbow's accurate range of 300 yards and potential rate of fire of 6 to 12 arrows per minute. However, in the post-feudal era of few standing armies, where a military force was likely to be composed of hastily trained peasants (Held 1970), the emphasis shifted from quality weapons to those which could be produced cheaply and quickly in large quantities.

While a bowyer (who had to be a highly skilled craftsman) might take two weeks to produce a longbow, and an hour apiece to make arrows, the hand gun, as well as enough shot for a major campaign, could be made by the average blacksmith in about a day (Hughes 1974). Even if the blacksmith and bower were paid equally well for their time, ten or more gunmen could be equipped as cheaply as a single archer.

Also, since the users of the weapons were going to receive little if any training or practice in their use, it is unlikely that they would be able to exploit the longbow's superiority. In any event, the rulers of the day evidently felt that a large number of cheaply equipped and poorly trained musket men would be more effective than a much smaller number of expensively equipped and trained archers. The conversion of European armies to the gun occurred because the gun was believed to be more "cost-effective;" the transition should not be construed as indicating that the gun's performance was comparable to that of the bow.

The first attempt to produce a gun which could be aimed resulted in the use between 1430 and 1460 of the five or six-foot-long "culverin." One man supported and aimed this 0.75 cal firearm while a partner fired it.

The Matchlock

By about 1440, possibly in Genoa, a firearm which permitted one man to aim, load, and fire was developed (Held 1970). In its many stages of evolution, this firearm is referred to as the "matchlock." The earliest matchlock was simply a hand cannon to which an eccentrically pivoted serpentine arm was fixed. A burning match was clamped to the top of the serpentine. The design was such that when the lower half of the serpentine was pulled toward the user, the glowing match-tip was lowered over the touch-hole. The touch-hole, on the top of the barrel, was usually bevelled inward somewhat so that this crude "flashpan" might be filled with priming powder to ensure ignition. I must mention at this point that while the early matchlock could be pointed with some accuracy, the weapon was not held to the shoulder and aimed in the manner of a modern rifle, but rather, was shot free-hand or held against the chest (Held 1970, Greener 1986, Wilkinson 1970).

The matchlock evolved slowly from 1450 to 1600. Among other refinements, a side-mounted flashpan with a cover was added and the sear-type lock was developed. Now the powder was not so likely to be blown out of the pan, or unintentionally ignited. The match holder was "cocked" in much the same way as a modern revolver and was forced into the pan by a spring when a trigger bar was pulled. A further improvement was effected by modifying the butt end of the stock such that the gun might be shouldered for firing.

Provided that the weather was dry and the wind light, the performance of the arquebus (as it came to be called) was doubtless impressive. It could be relied on to strike a man at 50 yards, perhaps even at 100, and the larger version of 0.75 cal or so could penetrate most armour at 40 or 50 yards.

While it is true that the matchlock was a widely used infantry arm after 1450, it is difficult to determine its relative effectiveness. All forces continued to use artillery and all continued to use a multitude of edged weapons in combination with the arquebus. As late as the 1800s musketeers were required to carry swords, while halberds, pikes, and other weapons were a part of every well equipped army. During the 1500s pikemen outnumbered musketmen, as they were necessary to protect them while loading, a slow and awkward procedure during which they had to

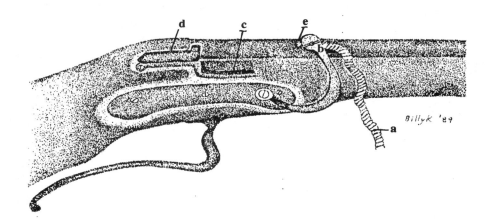

ILLUSTRATION ONE: A military-type matchlock musket circa 1700. This is the sort of weapon with which the European colonies were armed during the early seventeenth century. Typical military loading and firing drill involved about thirty-seven steps. It was necessary, first, to remove the lighted 'match' (a) from its clamp on the serpentine (b). Holding the match away from the firearm (and the powder container!) the musketman first poured a measured charge of powder down the barrel through the muzzle. This was followed by a wad of cloth or paper on which was placed the ball. This was rammed home using the ramrod to seat on the powder charge. Next, the weapon was 'primed' by pouring a small amount of (preferably fine-ground) gunpowder in the priming pan (c). The pan-cover (d) was moved over the pan to prevent the primer from spilling or being blown away (and also to minimize the possibility of accidental discharge). Next the match was replaced in the serpentine. To fire, the match was adjusted if necessary (they burn down and so require constant positioning) and was blown upon to ensure a brightly burning tip. The pan-cover was moved away from the pan to expose the primer, the weapon was shouldered (and possibly placed on a rest) and the trigger was used to release the spring-loaded serpentine which forced the lighted match into the priming pan. Provided that the match was burning well and that the priming powder was still there, and was dry, it would burn and, through the touch-hole ignite the main powder charge, the burning of which propelled the projectile.

remain erect. By 1600 most forces included pikes and muskets in about equal numbers (Hughes 1974). In 1597 the brilliant tactician Gustavus Adolphus formed the first army in which the arquebus was a predominant weapon, outnumbering pikes two to one (Hughes 1974). In 1631, however, the Swedish king's success during the battle of Breitenfeld was still deemed to have been contingent on the ability of the pikemen to stand fast. The pike was still in use during the early 1700s, and only became obsolete with the advent of bayonets.

Several estimates of the effectiveness of the arquebus have survived from a somewhat later period. In his *"L'artillerie au Debut des Guerres de la Revolution,"* Rouquerol estimates that under battle conditions 1/5 to 1/2 of

1 percent of the bullets fired hit their targets (Lauerma 1956, Hughes 1974). It was an only slightly facetious rule-of-thumb that in order to kill a man it was necessary to fire at him seven times his own weight in lead. William Muller (1811) estimates that at best, 50 percent of musket bullets could have been effective at 100 yards, assuming an optimistic misfire rate of 25 percent. Major Hughes (1974) bases an estimate on Muller's comments and other factors. He concludes that not more than 15 percent of shots fired could have been effective at 100 yards. At the end of this chapter I will deal with comparative musket performance in greater detail, and will outline relevant variables. In general, most improvements in military firearms technology between 1550 and 1800 concentrated on reliability and rate of fire. The accuracy of the smoothbore British Brown Bess, used as late as 1850, and that of the European musket of 1550 were likely comparable, given the same powder and ball.

By the late sixteenth century, the hand-held firearm had assumed standard sizes and shapes throughout the Continent and in England. For example, the Regulation of February 6, 1599 specified that light (.64 cal) and heavy (.80 cal) matchlocks were to be provided to the troops of the Dutch Republic. These specifications were roughly the same as those for "calivers" and "muskets" respectively in all European countries at this time. Firearms for civilian use followed the same general pattern as military firearms until the middle of the seventeenth century, differing mainly in ornamentation (Hughes 1974, Held 1970).

The most glaring fault of the matchlock was that a lighted match had to be carried at all times. It was necessary to light both ends as a safeguard against the accidental snuffing of one. It was not uncommon for arquebusiers to be caught without matches lit, rendering their weapons useless. In addition, the glow from the match made an easy target at night for an unseen enemy (Peterson 1956, Held 1970, Hughes 1974); even the smoke and odour from the match could reveal the user's whereabouts.

The loading procedure was an attempt to juggle match and powder so that they were as far away from each other as possible. Black powder is easily ignited, so much so that it was not uncommon for sparks from match or priming powder to ignite the string of bandoliers (each containing a single charge of powder) wrapped around the musketeer's neck, with disastrous results. The procedure for loading a matchlock required the following sequence:

1. Remove the match from its clamp;
2. Transfer musket and both ends of lighted match to one hand;
3. Open pan cover with the free hand;

4. Check to see that the touch-hole, the communication between pan and main charge, had not become obstructed (black powder fouls very quickly);

5. Open the bandolier or priming flask and pour a small charge of powder into the pan with the free hand;

6. Close the pan and blow loose powder blown off the piece;

7. Lower the butt of the firearm to the ground;

8. Pour the charge down the barrel with the free hand and return the bandolier to its place;

9. Remove the bullet from the pouch or the musketeer's mouth (Spanish sentries in America were required to keep balls in their mouths when on duty) (Peterson 1956) and place it in the muzzle of the musket over a cloth patch;

10. Withdraw the ram rod from its place underneath the barrel and push the ball smoothly down the barrel to seat solidly on the powder charge;[1]

11. Replace the ramrod;

12. Raise the gun, cradled in both hands;

13. Insert one end of the match in the clamp after it has been cocked;

14. Adjust the match so that it will fall squarely in the priming powder. If the gun was to be fired immediately, the user blew on the match to remove ashes and increase its heat, shouldered the piece, opened the pan cover, and pulled the trigger bar. If firing was delayed, it was necessary to "proportion the tow," that is, adjust the match which would burn down, such that it would again centre in the pan.

Considerable caution is advisable when loading, as burning embers from the last shot may remain in the barrel, and one is well-advised to angle the barrel away and to avoid exposing the hand directly over the muzzle.

---

[1] This could be a sensitive operation, especially with the meal powder of the 1600s (discussed later), for too much or too little seating pressure might drastically reduce the force of the shot. Even with today's corned powder, slight variances in seating pressure result in inconsistent muzzle velocities and consequent unpredictability of point of impact.

To avoid this latter problem, most authors advise waiting a full minute after a shot before reloading[2] (Nonte 1976, Ramage 1975).

It was not an uncommon practice, at least in Europe, to use a rest to fire the weapon, adding one more bit of paraphernalia to hamper the musketeer's loading. Further, it should be mentioned that the "gonne" of 1600, while being, in the case of the caliver, approximately the same weight and length as later firearms like the British Brown Bess or French Charleville muskets, was much more awkward to manipulate or fire. This is a difference which is better experienced through actual handling than description. The earlier muskets tend to be poorly balanced, usually front-heavy, and are shaped such that they feel most out of place when shouldered. Whereas a "modern" (*circa* 1725) firearm "fits" the shooter such that his line of sight is naturally along the barrel, it is necessary to bend the neck and lower the head with most of the older pieces. For this reason, I would suggest that, given identical performance potentials, the older musket would score fewer hits.

One need hardly describe the effect of rain upon the matchlock. Even if one could somehow load the piece with dry powder, the moment the pan was open to fire, water could dampen it and the shooter's hopes, if they had not already been extinguished along with his match.

The Wheelock

The earliest attempt to remedy the problems created by the necessity of having to carry a lighted match was a lock design which relied upon the sparks generated by holding a piece of iron pyrites against a spinning, serrated-metal wheel. The mechanism worked on the same principle as an older-type flint-and-wheel cigarette lighter. The top of the steel wheel filled a slot in the bottom of the priming pan. Suspended above the pan cover was a "cock," in the jaws of which was clamped the iron pyrites. Using a special wrench, the lock was "wound up," and the priming or flashpan filled (assuming the piece was charged with powder and shot). Some wheelocks were equipped such that the pan cover would automatically

[2] The value of this advice was demonstrated shortly before I began my period of range-testing. A shooter at the same range experienced a mis-fire with a 0.58 cal replica of a Remington Zouave musket which fires a bullet over one inch long, weighing nearly one and one-half ounces. Nonplussed by the failure of the gun to fire he placed its butt on the ground at his feet and then peered down the muzzle. His amused companions were then startled by the report of the gun's delayed discharge. Fortunately the shooter had finished his perusal of the bore and was looking elsewhere at the time.

open when the trigger was pulled, while with earlier or cheaper versions this operation was manually performed just before firing. In either case, when the pan cover was removed the cock with pyrites dropped into the pan in the midst of the powder, resting against the wheel. The rapid rotation of the wheel produced a shower of sparks which was usually adequate to ignite the powder in the pan and in turn the main charge.

Most authors feel that this weapon was primarily a toy of the wealthy and was rarely if ever issued to infantry. The extent of its military use appears to have been as a special purpose firearm, where the match was clearly inappropriate, as in the guarding of gunpowder, or similar duties.

Nevertheless, throughout the sixteenth and even seventeenth and eighteenth centuries the wheelock maintained a following. Those who could treat the gun gently and could afford to pay the price had the most sure and rapid firing gunlocks available, before the percussion system was developed in the 1800s. It should be emphasized at this point that while the village smith might repair a matchlock, a master gunsmith with experience with wheelock was required to repair one. Repairs often necessitated returning the piece to its maker in Nuremburg, Milan, Paris, or another large centre. In England, not a single gunsmith could produce an acceptable wheelock before 1650 (Held 1970), at which time the flintlock rendered it all but obsolete, at least as a military arm.

Until the end of the seventeenth century, most rulers chose to arm their infantry with matchlocks because the wheelock was so expensive (Greener 1986, Peterson 1956, French 1954, Hughes 1974, Held 1970, Wilkinson 1970). Where a matchlock light musket cost about $75 in today's currency, the plainest grade of wheelock would have cost about $300. In addition, where the matchlock was extremely rugged and could be repaired by any blacksmith, the wheelock was delicate and would require the regular services of a highly skilled gunsmith.

Gunnis Retinaculum Pyritae

Legend has it that Dutch chicken thieves, called "schnapphans" were the first to develop an affordable alternative to the matchlock. The technique of the day commonly used to light fires involved striking a piece of flint against one of steel. A gunlock which imitated this action evolved, probably by 1560, and was known by variations of the term "snaphaunce," or "pecking hen" lock. A piece of flint was clamped in the jaws of a "cock" not unlike the match holder of the matchlock. Approaching the pan from the opposite direction was an arm, to the end of which was appended a striking plate, the "frizzen." This was also referred to in various periods as the "battery," "steel," or "hammer."

To ready the snaphaunce for use the piece was charged, the pan filled with priming powder and its cover closed. Then the frizzen arm was lowered (moved rearward) over the pan. In early or cheaper examples, the pan cover was manually opened to fire, while many pans were automatically opened. To fire, the cock was pulled back until the sear "caught," fully compressing the mainspring. When the trigger was pulled, the cock snapped sharply forward, scraping the flint in a downward direction along the frizzen surface. The resulting shower of sparks falling into the pan served to ignite the primer, and thereby discharge the piece. Upon being struck by the cock, the frizzen was knocked up and away from the pan. The fall of the cock toward the flashpan was arrested by a buffer.

In Italy at about the same time a similar lock evolved; it is referred to as the Italian (as opposed to the Dutch type) snaphaunce. By the third decade of the seventeenth century this lock incorporated several features found in the more sophisticated "true flintlock." Where the Dutch version employed a partly internal sear, the nose of which protruded through the lockplate to hold the cock back against the mainspring by resting on its tail, the Italian or Brescian lock employed a fully internal sear. Instead of a "buffer" piece to arrest the fall of the cock, a "shoulder" was added to the cock itself for the purpose, stopping the fall when it came to rest against the edge of the lockplate. Further, the more advanced Italian snaphaunce was distinguished by the square shaft upon which cock and tumbler are mounted. The shaft is an integral part of the tumbler rather than the cock.

The features which distinguish the snaphaunce from all other flint guns are firstly the frizzen, which was mounted on the end of a manually positioned, hinged arm, and secondly the flashpan cover. This was always a sliding piece, not connected to the frizzen, and was usually opened automatically by a plunger driven by the falling cock.

The snaphaunce had most of the same advantages as the wheelock: no match was required, it was almost as fast in ignition and, in theory, it was as likely to fire. Further, it had some of the matchlock's advantages. The snaphaunce was much cheaper than the wheelock, and it was comparatively easy to build and repair. Flint is not friable like pyrites, and can be expected to yield showers of sparks as long as the edge is sharp (around 10–20 shots per flint). There is no wheel housing to become jammed by pyrites or fouled by powder residue, and no chain drive to break. The snaphaunce was also lighter and more compact. In rough usage, the main weakness of the snaphaunce was the relatively delicate frizzen-arm which might be easily broken or bent, and would not function in either case.

Unfortunately, the snaphaunce was destined to share the fate of the wheelock, primarily because it was still much more expensive than the matchlock. Between 1580 and 1650 millions of matchlocks were the standard equipment of all world armies (Held 1970, Wilkinson 1970, Hughes 1974). Robert Held also reminds us that:

> Neither gunlocks nor any new invention, school of thought, artistic movement or other innovation spread very fast in these times. There were few roads, and such as there were teemed with murderers, became ribbons of axle-deep mud in spring and turned into glaciers of snow and ice in winter. There was as yet no such thing as scheduled or public transportation . . . understandably enough, life was parochial when a hundred mile journey was fraught with vastly greater perils than a trip around the world today. Ninety-nine out of a hundred individuals died in the towns and villages in which they were born and never ventured more than twenty miles out of it in all their lives. The city a hundred miles away was a mysterious other world from which occasional sojourners brought tantalizing trickles of incredible tales of great cathedrals, palaces and countless citizens (rarely more than sixty thousand, most often fewer than twenty thousand) . . . Rhenish Gothic architecture was unknown fifty leagues away; Regensburger sausages were unheard of in Cologne; the manufacture of Venetian glass was inimitably the monopoly of that republic. The world was a complex sea of islands of peculiar native skills, traditions, customs, morals, religions, tongues, fashions and islands within islands, with not many routes of communion among them. (Held 1970:73)

While it is likely that knowledge of the latest invention would spread to "interested princes and worldly cosmopolites who lived on the plateaus of leisure and affluence . . . there the avenues of exchange stopped." A device invented in Utrecht in 1600 might easily "be a marvel of novelty in a French Hamlet or a Bavarian village twenty-five years later." (Held 1970:74)

Thus it was that in Spain, probably during the reign of Philip II (1556–98), another type of flint gun was developed, which shared features with the snaphaunce, ancestor of the flintlock. The "Miquellet" design or "Spanish lock" used the same sort of cock as its Dutch kin. There was, however, one most important refinement. The pan cover and the frizzen were combined in a single L-shaped piece. The piece pivoted at the toe, its upright section functioning as the frizzen while the horizontal part was the flashpan cover. A spur under the frizzen pivot exerted pressure on a feather spring, thereby holding the pan cover tightly closed. When the cock snapped forward, propelled by the mainspring, and struck the frizzen, its impact opened the pan cover about half way. When the spur underneath had pivoted past its focal point on the feather spring, the pan/frizzen snapped open the rest of the way. In this manner, the priming powder was automatically exposed to the shower of sparks created by striking the frizzen. This pan/frizzen combination was simpler and more rugged than the pan with opening mechanism and delicate frizzen arm used on the snaphaunce.

The Miquelet lock was *the* Spanish lock by the first quarter or half of the seventeenth century, and was so efficacious a mechanism that it was in use for over 250 years (Held 1970). In fact, no flint gun was developed until after 1760 or so which could be said to surpass it in reliability (Held 1970:26).

The cock of the Miquelet served as its own external tumbler, its mainspring being mounted on the outside of the lockplate. The mainspring pressed upward on a spur at the rear of the cock's base, save in the so-called southern Italian Miquelet (actually made mainly in central and northern Italy). With this later (around 1625) variation, the mainspring pulled down on a spur at the front of the cock. Most of these latter Miquelets were both highly sophisticated in execution and expensive, and therefore, as was the case with most advanced weapons, were seldom found in the hands of the poorer classes.

Sometime around 1610, probably in France, the best features of both Miquelet and snaphaunce were first combined to produce the "true flint-lock." Incorporating the L-shaped pan/frizzen of the Miquelet and the internal tumbler/mainspring mechanism of the snaphaunce, the flintlock was due to become the finest arm of its day, used widely by soldier and sportsman alike until the early 1800s.

The Jacobean Lock

While there is some considerable debate over precisely where the true flintlock first evolved, it does seem that the British were the first to make use of a rather clumsy version on a large scale. By 1630 the "Jacobean lock" was to be found throughout the British Isles. In 1638 the Scots, resisting the dictates of Charles I, possessed a number of Jacobean lock firearms, outnumbered, of course, by matchlock firearms (Held 1970).

The Jacobean lock was usually poorly proportioned and roughly constructed. The British had not yet mastered the finer points of flintlock craftsmanship that by 1703 were to allow the construction of the magnificent "Brown Bess."

At this point it will be useful to mention one of the critical elements in flintlock design. The ample shower of sparks upon which ignition depends requires that a delicate balance between mainspring and feather spring be achieved. The mainspring must propel the cock such that the flint will strike the frizzen and scrape along its surface with adequate force. Similarly, the feather spring which holds the pancover/frizzen closed, and which snaps open once it has pivoted about half way, must resist the cock strongly enough to produce the sparking, but must also allow the frizzen to be knocked away so that the spark may serve its purpose. Clearly it was necessary to balance both spring forces and leverages if the lock were to prove consistent in performance. In addition, if the steel of the frizzen were inadequately hardened, or were too hard, the action of the flint might fail to produce ignition (Held 1970, Wilkinson 1970, Greener 1986). All of these problems emerged during my test program, and are mentioned in Chapter Four. Thus the matchlock was more reliable and easier to make and continued its predominance until 1690–1700.

The Jacobean lock varied in its performance both among different samples, and at different times with the same one. When the flint struck the frizzen, it met with too little or too much resistance resulting either in misfire (and possible broken flint) or in a delay in ignition. The tendency of the ignition time to vary with even good locks considerably reduced accuracy. These problems remained in the 1800s as shown in this passage from the *Shooter's Guide:*

> It is of the utmost consequence to the excellence of a lock that the springs be proportioned to each other: if, for instance, the mainspring be very strong and the hammer/frizzen/spring weak, the cock will be liable to be broken for want of sufficient resistance to its stroke; on the other hand, if the hammer spring be stiff and the mainspring weak, the cock has not sufficient force to drive back the hammer; and, in both cases, the collision between the flint and the steel is too slight to produce the necessary fire. The face of the hammer also may be too hard or too soft; if too hard, the flint will make scarcely any impression upon it, and the sparks will be few and small; if too soft, the flint will cut into the hammer at every stroke, whilst the sparks will also be few in number and of a dull red colour . . . I prefer a lock, the springs of which are rather strong than otherwise, on account of its being less liable to miss fire. (Johnson, Thomas, London 1816)

Data on the misfire rates of seventeenth century flintlocks is unavailable. However, if locks were as variable as Johnson implies after an additional 150 years of development, the locks of the first half of the seventeenth century must have been capricious indeed!

The French Lock

If the British were the first to popularize the flintlock, the French were the first to produce a well made and refined version. It is sometimes difficult to credit an individual with the invention of a stage in the evolution of any technology. More likely, that set of refinements which comprise the true flintlock, like the ingredients of its propellant, were simultaneously combined by many "inventors."

For what it is worth, the French gunsmith, Mar le Bourgeoys is usually credited with the production of the first "true flintlock" around 1610–1615 (Brown 1976). It is likely that between 1625 and 1635 the first firearms incorporating this lock found their way to Paris (Held 1970).

The true flintlock incorporated a wholly interior mechanism, unlike the Miquelet, and a one-piece L-shaped flashpan cover/frizzen combination, unlike the snaphaunce. Those features which differentiate it from the Jacobean lock were primarily matters of refinement. Where the cock's fall was arrested by a screwed-on buffer piece in the case of the Dutch snaphaunce or English Jacobean lock, the true flintlock (like an Italian snaphaunce) had a shoulder on its inner side which struck the edge of the lockplate. The cock's configuration was the gooseneck, a shape it would retain for two hundred years. Whereas the sear of the Jacobean lock protruded through the lockplate and caught the rear of the cock, the flintlock employed an internal tumbler, which was mounted inside the lockplate upon the same shaft on which the cock was mounted. The sear, instead of protruding from the lockplate and catching the cock, was pivoted inside on a horizontal screw, and engaged successively two notches in the tumbler as the cock was pulled backward. The first of these notches was cut so deeply that no pull of the trigger could disengage the sear. This was the "safety" position, "half-bent" in the terminology of the time. The second or "full cock" notch was more shallow, such that the sear was easily forced out by the trigger. The frizzen piece was pivoted on its hinge so that it more readily achieved that delicate balance between too little and too much resistance to the cock (Held 1970, Johnson 1816, Greener 1986).

The French design, which modern collectors term the flintlock (as opposed to Miquelet or snaphaunce), was much more reliable and faster firing than its predecessors. This improvement can be attributed to refinements in design, metallurgy (Gordon 1959) and to a general improvement in craftsmanship. This latter occurred because the demand for more sophisticated firearms spawned the new trade of gunsmith. Where previously the matchlock firearms were serviced and even manufactured by blacksmiths or their equivalent, specific, complex skills were required to make or repair the new "firelocks." I stated earlier that the snaphaunce and Miquelet locks both worked very well (Held 1970, Greener 1986, Wilkinson 1970). Nevertheless, the Jacobean lock supplanted these older designs in England. Furthermore this lock did not work particularly well, as was probably also true of the other earliest true flintlocks. The flintlock only gradually became the standard firearm that it was by 1700 (Held 1970, Peterson 1956).

At first glance it would seem that crude and ineffective locks supplanted those which we know to be highly efficacious. How might this be explained? It is likely that the common grade of snaphaunce and Miquelet lock was very much inferior to the samples of these designs which are evaluated by weapons historians. Historians base their estimation of early flint-gun efficacy on examination of those few examples which remain in private collections or museums. Naturally firearms made more recently, after the advent of the flintlock, and finer grade weapons, were those more likely to be preserved, and are over-represented. Affordable snaphance and Miquelet locks were rare and did not work very well. It is likely that the Jacobean lock, despite its limitations, gained popularity because of the prohibitive cost of competing flint designs. The popularity of *all* flint guns soared during the 1600s, indicating a general improvement, not only in design, but also in execution. The true flintlock achieved primacy because it combined those two elusive qualities which comprise design excellence — it worked well and it was cheap to manufacture. I believe this point is critical, for otherwise we must believe that excellent flint guns were available during the early sixteenth century, and further, that they were replaced (at least in England) by much inferior weapons.

It was to be a very long time before the flintlock was duly exploited in war, paradoxically because at about the time of its genesis, guns, any guns, were to be needed more desperately than ever before. The Thirty Years War, beginning in Germany in 1618, so devastated European civilization that technological development of any kind ground to a virtual halt. The matchlock was the standard arm at the outbreak of the wars, and by 1625 those few gunsmiths available were much too busy to experiment with new designs. By 1635 there was barely time to render badly worn arms serviceable enough to re-enter the fray. Shortly after the wars began, sport shooting, traditionally the testing ground for new firearms, ceased almost entirely. The horrors of this period in European history are too well known to need recounting here. Suffice it to say that a land of famine, terror and utter hopelessness was unlikely to embrace any goal but survival, and could not afford the luxury of innovation (Held 1970). The Civil War in

England (1642–49) similarly curtailed firearms development in that country.

The flintlock then, between its invention and 1650, could be refined only in Italy, the Netherlands, and of course, France. Spain had only recently embraced and committed itself to the Miquelet, and while the Italians exuberantly developed and used the new device on wildfowl and each other, they did not begin to use it in military application until after 1675 (Held 1970:88).

There was no large scale adoption of the new lock in the Netherlands. This was perhaps because the Netherlands were not rich in game, and hunting not so popular a pastime (Held 1970:88). In addition, between 1590 and 1600, Prince Maurits of Orange instigated a far-reaching re-organization of the Dutch Republic's army which necessitated an enormous supply of more or less standardised firearms, obtained at first from Germany (Kist *et al.* 1974, Wijn 1934). The Regulation of 1599 (February 6) had specified two sizes of matchlocks as the standard arm (musket and caliver described earlier, on page 17). Having depleted the royal coffers, and stocked-up with matchlocks, the Dutch might be expected to receive coolly the suggestion that a new design be developed.

It should also be borne in mind that the Thirty Years War had an impact of a particular sort on the Dutch. As a result of the greatly increased European demand for arms, as well as the curtailment of firearms production in Germany (Suhl was destroyed by the Swedes in 1634), a major firearms industry developed in the northern Netherlands (raw materials for firearms production being readily available on the Dutch market) (Kist *et al.* 1974). By 1625, incredible quantities of Dutch arms were being exported. For example, between 1625 and 1627 the Danes bought 22,400 muskets; Russia acquired 50,000 muskets in 1630 through the merchant house of Trip alone, and an additional 12,500 in 1658 (Amsterdam Gemeente Archief in Kist *et al.* 1974). With such a demand for almost any gun the Dutch could produce in quantity, and no competition to speak of, there was little time or reason for innovation. During this period, however, the Dutch did make one extremely important contribution in their gradual standardization of arms. Bore sizes and weapons types became consistent, at least within a given army (Peterson 1956).

The earliest flintlock guns attributable to the Netherlands do not antedate the period 1630–1640, and were produced in the Maastricht region. The earliest recorded use of this weapon in the Netherlands was 1635 in the Limburg-Rhineland region (Kist *et al.* 1974).

The French were first to adopt the flintlock on a large scale. During the reign of Louis XIV, who assumed the throne in 1643 at the age of five, the flintlock developed rapidly as a military arm, such that it had gained general acceptance by 1660. In the period from 1660 to 1668 Louis equipped an army (five regiments) with them[3] and was the first European monarch to do so.

The flintlock may be said to have entered England with Charles II on his return from France in 1660. Many French firearms of finest quality were brought home by those who had shared the King's exile. Where English gunsmiths had been noteworthy mainly for their mediocrity, they now became the world's finest, a reputation they have retained.

The only way in which wildfowl might be killed with the matchlock, and to a lesser extent, the Jacobean lock firearm, was to approach the bird on the ground until the point that bird and shooter were roughly equidistant from the muzzle. The Jacobean lock was simply not consistent enough to permit shooting "on the fly." The English gentry adopted the French passion for wild-fowling, along with the first firearm with which the sport was feasible. The shooting of birds, formerly done on the ground by peasants seeking a meal, became the mania of the over-privileged. The patronage of the rich assured, British gunmaking entered its golden age.

Most historians base their assessment of the flintlock's efficacy on data from the eighteenth century, when the "Brown Bess" or "Charleville" muskets were the arms of empire in Europe. I must therefore mention the ways in which the muskets of the seventeenth century were inferior to the firearms used after 1700. The later weapons were, of course, stronger (Gordon 1959), and therefore could be loaded with heavier charges for greater range and lethality. More importantly, they were much more reliable and rugged. Let us examine them in greater detail.

The early flintlocks did not have a "bridle" on the tumbler. This was a flat plate which served as a bearing to keep the tumbler in perfectly verticle rotation, and prevented it from scraping or jamming against the lockplate. Without such a bridle, the force of the snapping cock can be drastically reduced by friction between the lockplate and tumbler. This problem alone could produce a one-in-seven misfire rate (Held 1970).

A second bridle was also missing on flintlocks made before 1700. This was a steel plate running from the outer edge of the flashpan to support the outside end of the screw upon which the frizzen pivoted. Where the screw was anchored only at one end, as on the earlier guns, it was likely to break or become bent, thus impeding or preventing altogether the action of the frizzen. Where a fully, or "double-bridled" flintlock such as the British "Brown Bess" (1703–1850) could be very reliable under ideal condi-

---

[3] According to Held (1970:88), these were "crude but operable military versions" of the true flintlock.

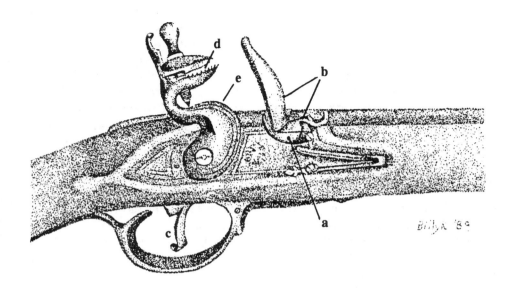

ILLUSTRATION TWO: A typical 'true' French-style flintlock. This example is a Grice lock, dated 1762 and mounted on a British Short Land Pattern musket, the much loved 'Brown Bess.' The French flintlock was designed about 1610 although it was not seen in the vicinity of Paris until about 1630. To load and fire, the musketman first pours a measured powder charge down the barrel through the muzzle. This is followed by a wadded ball, and as in the loading of the matchlock, this is rammed home with the ramrod. Next, the pan (a) is primed as with the matchlock. Then the combined frizzen/pan-cover (b) is rocked back to cover the pan. The weapon is now ready to fire. When the trigger (c) is pulled the spring-loaded cock (e) is driven forward, forcing the flint (d) to scrape along the frizzen. At the same time the flint's impact forces the combined frizzen/pan-cover (also spring-loaded) forward, thus exposing the priming-powder to the shower of sparks created by the friction of flint against steel. If the shower of sparks is adequate and the primer dry it will burn and ignite main charge.

tions, the same could not be said for the crude, unbridled guns of the seventeenth century.

Why Improve Locks But Not Accuracy?

It will be apparent to the reader that this chapter has dealt almost exclusively with firearm ignition systems, paying much attention to reliability and rate of fire, and little to range and accuracy.

During the period 1500 to the early 1700s and even up to the period preceding the American Revolution of 1776, most firearms development concentrated on improving reliability, concomitantly increasing the speed with which the piece might be loaded and fired. During the sixteenth century, it was known that "screwed" or rifled barrels greatly increased accurate range (Held 1970, Greener 1986, Peterson 1956), but this innovation (which imparted a spin to the projectile such that it would gyro-stabilize) was of little use in the context of European war. These battles tended to be of the open-field type in which massed musketeers fired at a massed enemy. The important thing was to fire as rapidly as possible. After all, it didn't really matter which of the enemy one hit. The British, especially, developed a complex of tactics based on rapid volley-fire by massed infantry followed by the bayonet charge. To facilitate rapid loading, ball and powder were carried in a paper package or cartridge. Because black powder fouled the barrel more with every shot, eventually preventing the ball from seating, it was desirable to use a ball somewhat smaller than the bore. This insured that the piece could be loaded, even after several shots had been fired. The Brown Bess of 0.75 cal was loaded with 100 gr of powder. A ball of only 0.69 cal literally rattled down the barrel, its point of impact being determined by the direction of the last bounce!

Rifles were used as early as the 1640s by both Cromwell and the Royalists (Held 1970), but were slow to load, and, because the ball had to fit the bore very tightly, could become unloadable due to fouling. The way to discover that a firearm is too badly fouled to be loaded is to ram the ball solidly about half to three quarters of the way down the barrel where it becomes solidly jammed. The fouling is always thicker near the breech. If there is more than an inch of airspace between powder and ball the piece will burst if fired (Held 1970, Wilkinson 1970, Hughes 1974), and the only remedy is to attempt to draw out the ball with a "bullet screw." This operation is best undertaken when the shooter is calm or, at any rate, not being shot at.

Even if the rifle bore was cleaned often enough that fouling did not become a problem (itself a time consuming operation), the firearm took a very long time to load. The ideal British infantryman of the period could, in theory, load and fire 4 shots per minute (Darling 1970, Held 1970) while, for example, the Jaegar rifle of 1700 (from which the "Kentucky rifle" evolved) could be loaded in 15 minutes (Greener 1986).

Contrary to popular Revolutionary War myth, many of the Americans who hid behind rocks firing at the massed "Redcoats" with their Kentucky rifles ended their attack impaled on British bayonets: the Americans required at least three minutes to ready for a second shot, the British, little more than half a minute. True, the rifle was as accurate at 200 yards as was the musket at 50, but a man can easily run 150 yards in twenty seconds. While fifty riflemen could fire a total of one hundred rounds at an enemy position every six minutes, the same number of musketeers could fire from 900 to 1,200 rounds. And with a massed target, the difference in effect between accurate and inaccurate fire was minimal (Hughes 1974:85, Held 1970). During the seventeenth and eighteenth centuries the effect of small arms fire was entirely dependent on the standard of fire discipline in a unit. If fire could be opened at 60 yards or less, its effectiveness must have been remarkably high — it seems that highly trained, professional armies of the eighteenth century could hit with 10 to 20 percent of the shots ordered to be fired (Hughes 1974:85).

Range was also reduced by the extreme "windage" (the difference between projectile and bore size), and was sacrificed in the interest of rate of fire (Hughes 1974, Greener 1986, Held 1970, Wilkinson 1970).

These considerations were relevant to gunners in Carolinian and Cromwellian times as evidenced by the 1/24-inch difference between their bore diameter and projectile size.[4] It was not until the invention, before the American Civil War, of the expanding "Minnie bullet" that a rifled firearm became practical (Hughes 1974, Held 1970, Greener 1986). Both sides of the American Revolutionary War used muskets of the same type.

The preceding inventory of technological development may seem at this point to be unnecessarily long and detailed. This introduction was necessary to acquaint some readers with the technology itself and to underscore the practical significance of seemingly minor design changes. Further, an appreciation for the 250-year history of gun use in Europe prior to its introduction in North America is necessary if we are to fully understand that European and Native perceptions of the firearm were bound to be radically different.

The gun, and tactics relating to its use, evolved as components of a particular tactical complex. Estimates of the utility of any artifact must always be context-specific. With an appreciation for the technological and tactical antecedents of the weapons systems which New World colonists brought in both their heads and hands, we are in a better position to interpret and understand the significance of their comments. As I suggest in Chapter Five, these individuals carried with them into a novel physical and social environment not only tools which had evolved to cope with a different set of conditions, but cognitive baggage as well. At times, both were maladaptive and were eventually discarded or modified. Europeans came to North America with a different set of expectations of war, not only with regard to tactics, but also its purpose, and the contingencies of victory or defeat. Europeans knew that armour, edged weapons, pikes and arquebuses were effective on European battle fields. Their expectations

---

[4] This may be compared to 1/20 inch in later times.

that the same weapons and tactics would be effective in North America were understandable but wrong.

Chapter Three

Colonial Arms

I have attempted, where possible, to use archival material in this study of colonial armament. *The Jesuit Relations* (Thwaites 1896–1901) and Champlain's writings (Biggar 1922–36) provide no lists of arms but do give us a good idea of the part they played in European/Native interaction. A great deal more information is available regarding English armament, and hence a longer and more detailed treatment is possible. Unfortunately, much of the Dutch material has been lost, sold for scrap in Holland, or destroyed by the 1913 fire at the New York State Historical Archives in Albany.

The paucity of archival information precludes a detailed description of weapons types used in New Holland, although some authors (for example, Tooker 1963, Otterbein 1965) have based their analyses upon speculation regarding the nature and volume of the Dutch gun trade. In fact, we simply do not know whether the Dutch colonists had large numbers of surplus weapons available to trade or what types of firearms they were.

Types of Muskets

The matchlock arquebuses with which all of the early colonists were armed were heavy and cumbersome, and they required a rest to support the barrel while firing. Awkward and slow to fire, they were even slower to reload. Because they were difficult to aim, they were inaccurate, especially when used against moving targets (Held 1970, Hughes 1974).

With only one exception (Otterbein 1965), writers concerned with this period (for example, Hunt 1972, Trigger 1976, Russell 1957) believe that matchlock weapons would have been of little use to Native people for their style of warfare.

The flint gun, on the other hand, could be loaded and readied to fire in as little as thirty seconds. It could be carried with the cock in the "half bent" position, so that the user needed only to move it back to full cock and pull the trigger to fire.

This weapon was the first and only firearm of the period which could have been useful to the Natives, and which they (recognizing this) were willing to purchase (Trigger 1976:431).

Therefore, when we discuss European firearms as a locus of trade-dependence (for example, Hunt 1972, Tooker 1963) or as an explanation for the victory of one tribe over another (Tooker 1963, Otterbein 1965), we are primarily concerned with the flint gun (Russell 1957:10). Thus in this chapter we examine the likelihood that the colonists were in a position to provide this type of weapon to their Indian trading partners before the Iroquois defeat of the Huron between the years 1648 and 1652.

The Colonists' Weapons

By 1600, settlement in the New World by the Spanish, French, English, Dutch, and Swedes had begun. After the failure of Sir Walter Raleigh's colony at Roanoke Island (1585–89), the British established their first foothold at Jamestown Island in 1607, one year earlier than the first French settlement at Annapolis Royal. The English colonies multiplied with great rapidity, starting with New England, and filling in all the space between their settlements, with the exception of the territory held by the Swedes and Dutch. The former settled in the lower Delaware Valley, western New Jersey and eastern Pennsylvania and the latter in New Amsterdam.

Hostilities involving indigenous populations began almost immediately (Peterson 1956, Jennings 1975), and from 1565, when the Spanish massacred the Huguenots in Florida, until 1763, when England defeated France in America, there was always war or fear of war among the Europeans.

To enter such a hostile environment all of the early colonists armed themselves as well as the technology of the day and their finances would permit. Preparing for war as they knew it, they brought body armour, swords, pikes and other edged weapons, heavy ordinance, and hand-held projectile weapons such as crossbows, and arquebuses. The military men among them had received their training on European battlefields, and brought with them the tools appropriate for this type of warfare. Thus, a large percentage of the earliest settlers were armed with pikes and similar pole-arms instead of projectile weapons (Peterson 1956).

In Europe, where specially trained segments of the population met in open fields to fight pitched battles, these weapons were appropriate.

Unfortunately, the weapons and the tactical complex in which they were components did not suit a situation where the whole White population was outnumbered and continually on the defensive. Wars consisting of ambushes, forays, and surprise attacks at night or in the rain demanded different tactics and military hardware.

The Spanish were the first to discover that their technology was inappropriate. The arquebus was cumbersome and slow, so much so, that in the minute it took to load, an Indian could approach within easy range, fire five arrows, and move out of range.

> They [the Indians] never stand still, but are always running and traversing from one place to another: by reason whereof neither crossbow nor arquebus can aim at them: and before one crossbowman can make one shot, an Indian will discharge three or four arrows; and he seldom misseth what he shooteth at . . .

Nor were aboriginal weapons ineffective. The same author, who accompanied de Soto, continues:

> An Indian arrow, where it findeth no armour, pierceth as deeply as a crossbow . . . those of cane do split and pierce a coate of maile and are more hurtfull than the other. (Gentleman of Elvas in Hackluyt—trans. 1609)

In one battle over a hundred Spanish died by these "primitive" weapons, while in one party alone eight harquibusiers were killed, and four wounded. Similarly, the French suffered high casualties in battle with the Timuccuans who killed two and wounded twenty-two in a single skirmish. The French attributed this success to the Natives having learned to shoot their arrows at areas of the body which were unprotected by armour (Covington 1975:23, 20).

Over the period covered by this study we can trace a gradual shift from weapons and tactics appropriate in the context of the European pitched battle to those suited to highly mobile "flying warfare" (Mather 1972) consisting in surprise attacks by small, highly mobile and relatively self-contained military units. This change, however, was gradual, with body armour being retained well into the 1640's (Brown 1898:625, 626, Shurtleff 1853:I:25, 26, Acts Orders, and Resolutions of the General Assembly of Virginia 1915:231).

The matchlock was very poorly suited for Indian style "guerrilla" warfare, a fact of which the Natives were cognizant. They therefore insisted on trading only for flint guns (Trigger 1976). For this reason, the presence of significant numbers of these weapons in a colony was a necessary (though not sufficient) precondition for the trade of guns to the Natives. It is therefore necessary to determine the dates at which there were sufficient flint guns available for trade to the Natives.

The Iroquois, with whom we are primarily concerned, traded mainly with the Dutch and English, while their enemies, the Huron, were involved with the French trade. We will examine the state of armament of each of these groups of colonists in turn.

The French

New France was always a trade-oriented community. The fur trade was of critical importance because only the land along the St. Lawrence River was suitable for agriculture. The St. Lawrence, with its access to the Great Lakes, was the perfect conduit to vast territories that promised a seemingly endless supply of peltries. In order to draw on these resources the French negotiated alliances with the Ottawas, the Illinois, the Huron and many other Native tribes. French trade always depended on long and vulnerable supply lines and a delicate balance of alliances with the Natives; consequently, the French were always in danger of losing the fur trade to their British competitors.

The French arrived in North America armed primarily with match-lock weapons. While very efficient wheelocks were available, only the wealthy, like Champlain himself, would have been able to afford them. Not only were the French suppliers of trade goods to the Huron, but they also introduced the Iroquois, albeit unpleasantly, to European weaponry.

In 1609, Champlain, along with his Indian allies, attacked a group of Mohawk in the "Battle of Lake Champlain." It would appear that the Mohawk were totally unprepared for their strange new enemy. Champlain fired one shot (four balls) from his arquebus which he claims hit three Iroquois chiefs. A second Frenchman then fired from concealment, and, after discharging some arrows, the Mohawk fled (Biggar 1922–36:2:99). From Champlain's illustration it is impossible to tell what type of firearm he was equipped with. One year later, on June 19, 1610, Champlain again attacked the Mohawk, at the Richelieu River. This time Champlain's sketch appears to depict at least one matchlock weapon (see illustration three, page 37).

However, the shock of their introduction to European civilization had apparently worn off, for the French nearly exhausted their ammunition without sign of surrender or flight on part of the Mohawk. The guns did frighten the Mohawk at first, but they soon began dropping to the ground to avoid being hit. Champlain and his followers eventually stormed the fort with swords and Native weaponry, and killed all but fifteen of the inhabitants (Trigger 1976:258).

ILLUSTRATION THREE: Detail from Samuel de Champlain's sketch "Battle of the Richeliew River," June 19, 1610. National Archives of Canada/NL-15318.

In 1615, Champlain attacked the Mohawk in their own territory. Whether this encounter represented victory or defeat in Native terms (Trigger 1976:314) is a moot point for the present discussion, although Champlain clearly interpreted it as the latter (Biggar 1922–36:3:66).

Trigger (1976:339) suggests that fear of French muskets resulted in fewer Iroquois raids between 1615 and 1624. I have difficulty accepting this suggestion in view of the meagre arsenal at Champlain's disposal. The French leader would certainly agree with me, as he was continually trying to convince Louis XIII that Quebec was under-gunned (for example, Biggar 1922–36:5:53). These efforts were not in vain, for on February 24, 1621 his sovereign wrote to say that arms and ammunition would be sent. The same year "2 arquebuses with wheelocks, from five to six feet long; 2 others with matchlocks of the same length; 523 lb. of good match and 187 more that was rotten" (Gooding 1962:21) arrived. These weapons were added to the existing stock, and were included in the first complete list we have, which was made by the British privateers who captured Quebec in 1629. The captured goods included: 14 muskets, 1 arquebus, 2 large wheelock arquebus 6–7 ft., and 2 matchlocks of same length.

This list represents an increase of only fifteen guns over the original number supplied to the expedition in 1621 and includes the arms of both the fort and the settlement (Gooding 1962:21). Surely the Iroquois nation, capable of fielding at least two thousand armed men (Snyderman 1948:57) could not be so easily cowed by so few Frenchmen whose most important fortress was incapable of arming a respectable raiding party, and would have been left completely defenceless had they done so.

We cannot be sure at what point the French began to acquire flint guns, but it is likely that they lagged behind the other colonists. Whereas the English and Dutch used early designs such as the snaphaunce of Jacobean locks, these were never popular in France (Gooding 1962:22). The "true flintlock" which they did adopt could not have been generally available until the 1640s at the earliest.

There is record of Champlain presenting a gun of a new type to a Native as early as 1641. Gooding (1962:22) suggests that this may have been a flintlock. Unfortunately it could as easily have been a wheelock, as this type would also have been wholly new to the Natives. We can be quite certain, however, that trade of a few guns to the Natives was possible (Thwaites 1896–1901:25:27). We have no accurate information regarding the volume of weapons trade which French supplies could have supported. As the number of Huron who were Christian converts and therefore permitted to buy guns was quite small, minimal French surpluses would have been sufficient to supply all potential customers.

It is apparent by 1653 that the refugee Huron and their allies, the Ottawas, expected that large numbers of guns could be acquired from the French (Thwaites 1896–1901:40:213–25).

The French refusal to sell guns to non-Christians in the period before Huronia was destroyed is probably more significant than any lack of supply of these weapons after 1643 (Tooker 1963). However, we can only speculate about what the volume of this trade might have been had the ban been lifted before the decisive Iroquois attacks.

The English

The English colonies dotted the Atlantic coast and all participated in the fur trade. By 1640, British incursions into Indian territories had provoked war in Virginia (1622) and New England (the Pequot War of 1636–37). By 1675, several tribes and all of the New England British were engaged in a protracted and brutal struggle which came to be known as King Philip's War. Both Britain and France extended their European competition through alliances with Natives, inciting them to attack both the imperial adversary and their Native allies. This antagonism eventually resulted in the French and Indian War of 1754–63 in which Britain gained the upper hand, only to almost lose it during Pontiac's rebellion of 1763.

The English arrived armed with matchlock weapons. Even the higher ranking members of the early settlements used this type of weapon. For example, Captain John Smith, whom one might expect to have been well armed, was seriously burned in 1609 when his match ignited the powder in his pocket (Peterson 1957:19).

The Martial Laws of Virginia (1611), specify the duties of a sentinel as follows:

> ... he shall shoulder his piece, both ends of his match being alight, and his piece charged, and primed, and bullets in his mouth, there to stand with a careful and waking eye, until such time as his Corporall shall relieve him. (William Stratchey 1612)

The matchlock predominated as a military gun throughout the seventeenth century in England, being retained by the army until the reign of William III, who died in 1704. The change to the less awkward flint guns began early in North America, as might be expected of a frontier area. Their use as early as 1620 is evidenced by the account of a surprise attack on William Bradford and Edward Winslow's party of Pilgrims: "Captain Miles Standish, having a snaphaunce ready, made a shot, and after him another, after they two had shot, other two of us were ready ... there were four only of us which had their arms there ready." The men then turned their attention to their companions at their shallop: "wee heard three of their peeces go off, and the rest called for a firebrand to light their matches ..." (Bradford and Winslow 1969:53). Although several flint guns (the specific use of the term "snaphaunce" is a modern convention) were in evidence, it is clear from Bradford and Winslow's narrative that these were a minority: "[We] kept a good watch with three sentinels all night, every one standing when his turn came, while five or six inches of match was burning." (Bradford and Winslow 1969:24); "Then we lighted all our matches and prepared ourselves concluding we were near their dwellings." (Bradford and Winslow 1969:32).

The Pilgrims were also well provided with other armament of their day: "wee were so laden with armour that we could carry no more" (Bradford and Winslow 1969:22). Sixteen Pilgrims set out to reconnoitre, including their commanders, Miles Standish, Bradford, Hopkins, and

Tilley, each equipped with a musket, sword, and a corslet (Bradford and Winslow 1969:13). A soldier was not fully dressed in 1620 without his "piece, a jock, coat of maile, and a sword or rapier." In fact, armour remained in fashion for some time. In 1629 in a record concerning the Salem colonists there appears note of an agreement with an armourer in London: ". . . for twenty arms, namely, corset, breast, back, culet, gorget, tasses, and head piece to each . . . four of which are to be with close head pieces." These same colonists also ordered accessories for their guns: "Forty bandillers of neat's leather in broad girdles with boxes for twelve cartridges." (Cheever 1848:363).

By far the best armed English colony was Virginia, where in 1624–25 a complete military census was taken. Ideally the list below would include the total armament of the 1,209 Virginians. It is important to note that 940 of these inhabitants were male. The census included 19 settlements, ranging in size from 8 to 198 individuals (Wariscoyack and Elizabeth City, respectively). This colony possessed:

Armament	Total for colony
"Pieces of ordinance"	20
swords	429
coats of mail and headpieces	260
armour complete	342
pistols	55
matchlocks	47
"Peeces fixit" and snaphaunces	981
shot	9,657 lb
powder	1,129 3/4 lb

[Brown 1898: 610–27]

From this list, it would appear that the colony could, by 1625, have armed most men with "peeces fixit" or snaphaunces, even if we allow that a considerable number of these weapons were likely to be in need of repair. Approximately one half of the males could be armed with swords, one third could wear "armour complete," and one quarter might have been equipped with coates of mail and headpieces.

The ammunition figures raise some interesting questions. Even if we do not allow for the inevitable spoilage, the colonists were in possession of only 1.2 lb of powder per man. Allowing that muskets of 0.65 to 0.75 bore require about 100 gr. of powder per shot (see Chapter Five) it would appear that under ideal conditions (that is to say, zero wastage or spoilage) this arsenal permitted only 120 shots per man. As this census likely included a majority of arms and supplies intended mainly for hunting as well as defence, the colony seems pitifully under-armed. Two days of European-style volley fire could easily have exhausted an individual's munitions.

John Smith would agree with the above. He tells us that ten pounds of powder per man was thought to be necessary provision in Maryland. In 1635, a decade after the Virginia census, Smith tells us that each adventurer was to be equipped with a matchlock musket, as is evident from the list of supplies below:

- Item, one musket
- Item, 40 pounds of Lead, Bullets
- Pistoll and Goose shot of each sort some
- Item, one sword
- Item, one belt
- Item, one bandeleere and flaske
- Item, in[ch] Match

[John Smith, "A True Relation of Maryland" (1907:94)]

Lest the reader be misled by the 1625 Virginia figures, I must refer to Chapter Two where I suggest that the flint gun, in the form of what we now call the snaphaunce or Miquelet, had been around for some time by this date, and also that these weapons were not the functional equivalent of "modern" flintlocks. It follows that many of the guns listed in the census were old and unusable and that those which were operational would not remain so for long in hard use.

The British who captured and held Quebec from 1629 to 1632 would, we might assume, have been optimally equipped. Facing danger of attack from the French and the Indians, they had good reason to be battle-ready. Their supplies included:

Item	Probable Type
75 muskets	matchlock
25 fowling pieces	quite possibly snaphaunce or Jacobean lock
30 pistols	either wheelock or early flint
10 arquebuses-a-croc	a two-man wall gun

[in Gooding 1962:22; the identifications are my own]

The above, while representing a seven-fold increase over Champlain's armament, was only barely adequate to defend a fort and arm a small raiding party. As the above list is the total number of weapons supplied to Quebec from 1629 to 1632, and as the English traded some matchlock guns to the Montagnais (Thwaites 1896–1901:6:309), we may safely assume that even they were more poorly armed than it would first appear.

If the English at Quebec were armed primarily with matchlock weapons, despite their rather tenuous military position, it is no surprise that their countrymen to the south were similarly armed. While some colonies, notably Virginia and Massachusetts, adopted the flint gun for military and hunting use (Brown 1828–1912 [1898], and Shurtleff 1853–54:I:25:26), the matchlock, for reasons of availability, economy, simplicity, ease of repair, and reliability, continued in use well into the mid-seventeenth century.

During a general meeting on March 13, 1638, the Rhode Island colonists, probably reflecting concern as to what the aftermath of the Pequot War might bring in terms of relations with other, much larger and closer, Native groups, made the following ruling: "It is ordered that every Inhabitant of the Island shall be always provided of one muskett, one pound of powder, twenty bulletts and two fademe of match, with Sword and rest and Bandeliers, all completely furnished." (Bartlett, 1856:I:54)

In this period, it is apparent that where lock types are not specified (for example, matchlock, firelock, snaplock), the term "musket" generally refers to a military arm of a matchlock type. The term "fowling piece" refers to a civilian weapon, usually, but not necessarily, of lighter weight and smaller bore, equipped with some sort of flint lock. Thus, we may assume that the following order of the General Court of New Haven, November 25, 1639, refers to matchlock weapons: "It is ordered that every one that bears armes shall be compleatly furnished with armes (viz.), a muskett, a sworde, bandaleers, a rest, a pound of powder, 20 bullets fitted to their muskett, or 4 pound of pistoll shott or swan shott att least . . ." (Hoadly 1857:25:26). Should confirmation be needed that the above refers to heavy military, and therefore matchlock weapons, the requirement of "a rest" provides it.

Our main source of data for Connecticut during this same period is personal estate inventories. The following are representative:

1640 J. Olmstead: • 1 pike
- 1 corslet
- 3 muskets (matchlock)
- 1 fowling piece [probably flint gun, eg. Jacobean]

- 3 pair bandoleers
- 1 sword
- 1 rapier
- 1 dagger
- 3 rests [used for heavy military matchlocks]
- 2 pistols [flintlock or wheelock]
- powder
- shot
- match

Will Spencer:
- 1 musket
- bandoleers
- 2 swords
- 1 fowling piece [probably flint gun]

Thomas Johnson:
- 1 musket
- 1 sword
- bandoleers
- 1 rest

[Hoadly 1850–1890:I:448,449,451,453; the identifications are my own.]

When one Mrs. Hutchinson and her followers in the Massachusetts Bay colony were subjected to religious persecution by their fellow Puritans during the Antinomian crisis in the late 1630s, and disarmed to prevent resistance, the following types of weapons were confiscated:

- pistols
- swords
- powder
- shot
- match

[Winthrop 1972:206–208]

The match mentioned above could have only been for use with long guns, which are not listed (see Chapter Two).

On October 10, 1643 the General Court at Plymouth required that all citizens have a musket of either firelock (flint) or matchlock type. Also mandatory was the acquisition of match, a pair of bandoliers or a pouch for powder and bullets, a sword with belt, a rest, and shooting accessories, such as a bullet worm (Shurtleff and Pulsifer 1855–1861:II:65). Again, the requirement of a rest indicates that the Court anticipated that the majority of weapons would be of the heavy, military type. Such weapons in this period were invariably matchlocks. One year later, Virginia armed a large party, allowing each man:

- 4 lb. bullets (either lead or pewter)
- 1 lb. powder
- 1 "good fixed gunne"
- some defensive coat or armour and head piece
- a sword or cutlass

[July 1, 1644 "Acts, Orders and Resolutions of the General Assembly of Virginia" 1915:231]

This level of armament was far from universal among the English, for the colonists who were killed by Indians at Pavonia in 1643 "had only one gun among them." (Van Laer 1974:57a:128–29) We must remember also, that the guns to which these records refer are likely to be of the Jacobean type, and consequently less effectual than later flint guns.

Most of the English colonists were, it seems, only beginning to replace the tried and true matchlock during the 1640s. Their problem was partly one of limited supply. During the 1640s, King Charles I and Oliver Cromwell were engaged in a military struggle which left few surplus weapons available for export. When the homeland was pressing every conceivable form of weapon into service it is not surprising that English weapons stocks in the New World changed little.

The British conversion to flint guns was slow, but was well under way by 1666 when the General Assembly of Maryland voted to acquire a small number of them:

> Voted necessary that there be . . . [140] Snaphance Musketts high Caluver bore 140 Cutlashes and Belts fifty Carabines for Horsemen two dozen Bullettmolds high Caluver bore and two dozen of Carabine Bullet Moulds to be equally distributed into the several Countys of this Province when purchased to remain there in the Charge and Custody of such person or persons as the Lieut. General . . . shall appoint . . . (Brown 1828–1912 (1884):II:19–20)

Much later, in the period 1692–1702, New Hampshire required militiamen to be provided with: "a well fixed gun or fussee [a term used to denote a flintlock, indicating that 'gun' might mean a matchlock], Sword or Hatchett, Snapsack, Courtouchbox, horne, charger and flints, with six charges of powder . . ." (Bouton 1867–1941:III:178).

We must remember, of course, that such legislation takes some time to have an effect. The state of armament envisioned by the legislators may not have been achieved for many years, or may not have been realized at all. It would appear that by the time of King Philip's War of 1675–76 the majority of militiamen were equipped with some sort of flint gun (Peterson 1956, Brown 1976).

The data are not sufficiently detailed to enable us to establish the point at which the English first possessed a surplus of flint guns such that some could have been traded to the Indians. We can, however, be quite sure that such a state had not been reached by the 1640s.

The Dutch

The Dutch colonists, like their French and English counterparts, arrived in North America carrying swords and matchlock guns, and wearing armour. At least in the beginning, there is no evidence at all that they had wheelock or flint weapons. For example, Henry Hudson and his men are reported to have fared badly in an encounter with Indians in 1609 when all their matches were extinguished by rain (Robert Juet in Franklin 1959:19).

While some flint guns were to be found among the English colonists (Bradford and Winslow 1969) by 1620, it is likely that the Dutch lagged behind. The Dutch supply problems were due to the Thirty Years War. They were exporting guns to other European countries as quickly as they could produce them, and were not motivated to innovate. Flintlock weapons began to be produced in the Netherlands about twenty or thirty years later than in France. It follows that relatively few of these weapons would find their way to the American colony, and it was unlikely that such weapons were imported in quantity from other European sources.

The colonial administration even tried to ban the importation of flint guns in 1656, permitting the settlers to bring only matchlock guns into New Holland (Russell 1957:10). Had the matchlock been considered obsolete and the conversion to flint guns fairly complete, such legislation would not have made sense. Further evidence that the Dutch had by no means replaced their own matchlocks until well after the destruction of Huronia may be found in the following armament lists.

In 1656, the following supplies were considered necessary for the 150-man force which was to march against the Swedes on the Delaware River in New Netherlands:

- 75 muskets (matchlocks)
- 75 firelocks or snaphaunces
- 75 bandoleers
- 75 cartridge boxes
- 75 swords
- 75 hangers
- 75 sword belts
- 75 sabre belts
- 2,000 lb powder
- 600 lb lead
- 400 lb musket balls

[O'Callaghan 1853–87:I:645; the identifications are my own.]

It is likely that this list represents optimal armament for a force which was expected to encounter difficulty, rather than an average for the settlements. Similarly, in 1660 the Dutch list entitled "Return of Goods for the Colonie in the Delaware River" shows that both the matchlock musket and the flint snaphaunce were in use.

- 800 lbs powder
- 600 lbs musket and snaphaunce bullets [N.B., musket as opposed to flint gun]
- 40 snaphaunces
- Worms, priming brushes and
- flints in proportion
- 8 snaphaunce moulds
- 40 cartridge boxes
- 3 iron ladles to melt lead

[O'Callaghan, 1853–87:II:185]

It is clear that by the mid-seventeenth century, the snaphaunce and flintlock were perceived by the European colonists to be the most desirable military weapons. This is evident by the fact that this design completely replaced the matchlock in military use by approximately the year 1700

(Peterson 1956, Brown 1897:II:19–20, Bouton 1867–1893:I:80–81). Further, in consideration of the much higher cost of the flint gun, the decision by 1656 to include a sizeable proportion of these weapons as basic equipment is indicative of Dutch esteem for the design. We know also, that the matchlock was the most common arm in the possession of militiamen before 1675 (Leach 1958:12). Yet from the above examples it is evident that even as late as 1660, the Dutch, often cited as the Mohawks' main armourers, had by no means completed their own conversion to the use of those weapons which Tooker (1963), Trigger (1969, 1976, 1985:262) and Otterbein (1965) say they traded to the Indians.

Fully eight years after the major Iroquois attacks against Huronia (1648), the Dutch envisioned arming only half of an important force with snaphaunces. We are unable to determine whether even that modest goal was achieved. Surely common sense requires that we reconsider the suggestion that during the 1640s the Dutch were either able or willing to trade significant numbers of flint guns to Native people.

Later Colonial Armament

By 1660 all of the European colonies were moving to equip themselves with flint weapons. This trend may be attributable to greater availability of these weapons, as well as improvement in the quality of the available guns. Moreover, the settlers had learned that North American warfare required changes in tactics and equipment. To expect that it would take less than thirty or forty years to change patterns of thinking about warfare which had persisted for hundreds of years is surely expecting too much. Even modern military establishments invariably attempt to "fight their last war," applying lessons learned through past conflict in the context of present exigencies where such tactics may, in retrospect, seem ridiculously inappropriate (Chown 1977).

By 1700, the use of the flint gun seems to have been assumed. In 1701 Massachusetts required that militiamen equip themselves with flints as a matter of course (Boone 1701:73) while in 1702, Virginia received from Queen Anne 1,000 swords and 1,000 "Snaptice Musquets" for the arming of 1,000 foot soldiers. At the same time, 400 carbines and 400 pairs of pistols were received to arm 400 horsemen (Palmer and Flournoy 1875–93:I:80, 81).

The preceding references take us somewhat beyond the period on which I wish to focus, but are necessary in order to demonstrate that the flintlock cannot be assumed to have predominated in the colonies until well after the Iroquois/Huron war. During the first half of the eighteenth century, it was still deemed necessary to specify, rather than assume, that military guns were to be of flint design (for example, Virginia 1705, Connecticut 1741; see Hening 1971:III:338 and Hoadly 1850–1890:8:380).

Finally, the early trade in firearms between the colonists and Native peoples could not have been as extensive as has formerly been thought. Firstly, the colonists were barely able to arm their own populations during most of the seventeenth century. Secondly, the flint guns desired by the Indians were in short supply throughout this period (Leach, 1958 suggests 1675 as a cut-off date for matchlock predominance).

Where the colonies were apparently at pains to acquire a reasonable proportion of flint guns for their own military forces, it seems unlikely that the sale of such weapons outside of the community to potential enemies would be possible, or permitted.

Chapter Four

The Native/European Gun
Trade Before 1640

This chapter examines the evidence that Natives, trading with the colonists who supplied the Iroquois with guns, were using these weapons before 1640. This issue is important for two reasons. Firstly, Hunt (1972) and his followers use the premise that a large-scale gun trade developed at a very early date as a springboard to the assumption that the Iroquois became dependent on the use of guns before 1644. Secondly, these scholars assert that early seventeenth century muskets conferred a marked advantage upon their owners or, at least, that Natives believed that they did. Thirdly, compelling evidence regarding the period after 1644 is not available; it is therefore important to provide a comprehensive historical context for the evidence that does exist.

Although all European colonies prohibited trade in firearms to the Natives, it is equally true that these same colonists went to some pains to demonstrate the efficacy of their "peeces" to those same Natives (Covington 1975, Bradford and Winslow 1969:105,106,108, Trigger 1976). One might speculate that they were trying to convince themselves, as well as the Indians, that their superior technology gave them the upper hand (Fisher 1977:39). In his excellent work on European/Native relations in British Columbia in the period 1774–1890, Robin Fisher points out that even at this late date, some Indians were singularly unimpressed by the traders' bluster (Fisher 1977:39–40) and Finlayson tells us that the Natives explained patiently why their weapons were better than guns (Finlayson 1913:17). I suggest that the situation during early settlement on the east coast was similar in many respects, and Fisher's comments are applicable. The settlers were vastly outnumbered by well organized and integrated tribal groups possessing a sophisticated technology adapted to their shared environment. Secondly, the Europeans were rapidly encroaching on the territory of sedentary peoples who were militarily capable of utterly destroying them should they be motivated to do so (Jennings 1975, Fisher 1977). Unable to accept the notion that their continued presence in New England, New Holland, New France or New Sweden was subject to the indulgence of "capricious savages," the colonists had to create a myth of control, which persists in some forms to this day (I develop this argument further in Chapter Five). Fisher (1977:39) observes that west coast traders took every opportunity to stage demonstrations (under the most favourable conditions of course) of the power of their firearms, bragging about their offensive capabilities, should friend become foe, or some other offence be given them. We can only speculate about the effects such bluster might have had during the early contact period on the east coast. Whether or not the Europeans succeeded in convincing themselves or each other is unclear. Equally unclear is the impression that they made upon the Indians.

It is clear, however, that Native people had considerable experience of the firearms which Europeans possessed. The Mohawk were, perhaps, the earliest North American tribe to be exposed to hostile gunfire and they quickly developed strategies to defeat the new weapon (Trigger 1976:259, Biggar 1922–36:3:66). In 1620, Captain Miles Standish and his party of Pilgrims used guns to defend themselves against Indian attack in New England (Bradford and Winslow 1969:52), though this was by no means the Wampanoags' first contact with White men or their weapons (Bradford and Winslow 1969:84). I have dealt briefly with early French/Mohawk encounters elsewhere (Chapter Five) and will not repeat those arguments here. However, let us look more closely at the earliest recorded Native/English encounters.

During the aforementioned 1620 incident, it is apparent that the Indians used only bows and arrows while the English used only guns (Bradford and Winslow 1969:52). It is apparent from accounts of further events that no New England Natives encountered by the Pilgrims were in possession of firearms (for example, Bradford and Winslow 1969:95–96).

It should hardly surprise us when individuals, exposed to an obviously dangerous (and loud) "unknown quantity," are initially fearful and cautious. For example, Masasoyt's Brother Quaddequina quite naturally: ". . . was very fearful of our peeces and made signs of dislike that they should be carried away." And Masasoyt wanted English allies because: ". . . our peeces are terrible to them [Narowhiganseis] who are his enemies." For the reasons suggested above, the Europeans attempted to sustain that fear: "Whereat we called for our peeces and bid them not to fear; for though [the Narragansett] were twenty, we two alone would not care for them." Later,

"There we challenged them to shot with them for skins: but they durst not."
(Bradford and Winslow 1969:95–96, 105–108). The Natives, for their part,
quickly set about investigating the capabilities of these weapons. Bradford
and Winslow interpret Native unwillingness to compete as a sign that they
realized they could not. In light of what we know about the relative
accuracy of gun and bow I suggest that this was an ethnocentric (and
technically naive) interpretation of the Indian response. The Natives were
already aware that the gun was not infallible:

> . . . [The] Indian captain stood behind a tree within half a
> musket shot of us [perhaps 35 yards?] and there let his
> arrows fly at us; he was seene to shoot three arrowes which
> were all avoyded, for he at whom the first arrow was
> aymed, saw it and stooped down and it flew over him, the
> rest were avoyded . . . he stood three shots of a musket, at
> length one tooke as he sayd full ayme at him, after which
> he gave an extraordinary cry and away they went all. (Brad-
> ford and Winslow 1969:52)

Even this fourth shot was a miss, we hear from Morton's account of
the same incident, written in 1669. He reports that the "lusty savage" stood
three shots of a musket from within half a musket shot "until one taking
full aim at him, made the bark or splinters of the tree fly about his ears."
(Morton 1669:20)

The Natives had not yet had enough exposure to firearms to accurately evaluate them. Quite reasonably they preferred if possible to assess
the firearm without revealing more about their own weaponry than necessary. When challenged to a marksmanship competition, they declined.
The Europeans assumed that "they durst not" and that when "onely they
desired to see one of us shoote at a marke," (Bradford and Winslow
1969:108) their curiosity was innocent. Similarly, when Massasoyt re-
quested through Samoest "that at our meeting we would discharge our
peeces," the English do not indicate suspicion. Perhaps Massasoyt wished
to gasp in awe or perhaps he saw an opportunity to further evaluate this
armament, neutralizing the weapons at the same time. Perhaps "they durst
not" compete with the Europeans and naturally, "one of us going about to
charge his peece, the women and children through fear [ran away]." It also
seems reasonable that when, "one of us shoote at a mark, who shooting
with Haile shot, [the Natives] wondered to see the mark so full of holes."
(Bradford and Winslow 1969:106–108)

I too noticed that during the test phase of this project, others (including experienced range officers) tended to run for cover whenever I
"charged a piece." I too would use haile shot if I wanted to impress

someone, and knew there was no other way that my weapon was likely to hit the target.[1]

Though I discuss Native motivation for the acquisition of firearms in Chapter Eight, a tentative inventory of possible explanations is appropriate at this juncture. First, of course, the gun was a novelty, quite dissimilar to any device Indian technology had produced; it made an incredible "thunder," spewed forth "lightning," jumped wildly in the hands of its user, and sent forth "invisible" projectiles. In the event of a hit, the effect upon a solid target of a single ball was impressive. The prestige of owning such a novelty, regardless of its utility, would provide ample reason for becoming ". . . mad after them . . . [they] would not stick to give any price they could attain to for them: accounting their bows and arrows but baubles in comparison of them." (Bradford 1952:207) It is gratuitous to assume that Native attempts to acquire firearms reflected acknowledgement of superior weaponry. Firstly, it is clear that prior to the Pequot War very few groups of Indians had any chance to assess the weapons (Trigger 1976:630,431,264/1985:204, Trelease 1971:95, Bradford 1952:207). Secondly, we do not know what significance Natives ascribed to the articles bartered and received.

A weapons historian and collector whom I consulted in the course of this research advanced the usual argument that the Natives must have been militarily dependent upon European guns because they went to so much trouble to get them. As he spoke, my eyes strayed to the wall behind him, where he displayed a number of obsolete and unfireable firearms which he had proudly announced were worth as much as six thousand dollars apiece! Perhaps future ethnohistorians will argue that segments of the North American population in the twentieth century required Cadillacs or two-thousand-dollar mountain bikes. They will not, I hope, argue that the main reason was transportation! We do not know to what extent the gun as a symbol of European esteem would have been valued, even if it could not fire a projectile. Perhaps the unique ability of the musket, loaded with haile shot, to kill a small animal or a flying bird at some distance, was the facet of this technology of most interest to the Indians.

---

[1] I would also know that the lethality of my weapon was greatly reduced by the use of "haile shot." Both the power and range of multiple projectiles are dramatically less than those of a single ball. Hence it is unlikely that multiple-shot charges could pose a significant threat at any but the shortest range. Modern multiple-projectile small-arms systems use extremely effective gas seals and are still useless at long range; their effectiveness results from multiple impacts at short range, not from increasing the likelihood of impact.

This is the function which Bradford emphasized in his advice to new colonists:

> . . . bring every man a musket or fowling Peece, let your peece be long in the barrell, and feare not the weight of it, for most of our shooting is from stands . . . Let your shotte be most for bigge fowles and bring store of Powder and Schotte. (Bradford and Winslow 1969:141)

Another reason, unrelated to objective military efficacy, for acquiring firearms was the effect such ownership might have on the attitudes of tribes farther removed from contact with the newcomers. Not only might the gun itself impress, but the intercourse and alliance it symbolized would likely inspire some measure of respect, or at least caution.

The first group of Natives to acquire a number of firearms appear to have been the Montagnais. Champlain records that in 1620 two vessels from La Rochelle had illegally traded a large supply of weapons with powder and shot (Biggar 1922–36:5:3). Eustace Boulle, his brother-in-law, is cited in a *The Jesuit Relations* for 1621:

> He told us that two vessels from La Rochelle, one of 70 tons, the other of 45 had come close to Tadoussac for the purpose of trading, notwithstanding the King's prohibition . . . These people carried off this year a quantity of peltries and had given to the savages a large supply of firearms, with powder, lead, and match—a most pernicious and mischievous thing thus to arm these infidels, who might on occasion use these weapons against us. (Thwaites 1896–1901:32:147)

From the above, it is evident that the weapons were matchlocks. We have no reason to believe that these guns were of use to the Montagnais in warfare. We do know that these were not the only weaponry traded to Natives during this period. In his Royal Proclamation of November 6, 1622 James I prohibited unauthorized trade to New England because of those men "who did not forbear to barter away to the savages, swords, pikes, muskets, fowling-pieces, match, powder, shot and other warlike weapons, and teach them the use thereof." Charles I issued a similar proclamation in 1630.

As mentioned above, most European colonies were guilty of trading guns, and all blamed the others, not only for selling more guns, but indirectly, for the trade in which they themselves engaged. Thus, William Bradford, governor of Plymouth colony from 1627 to 1656, remarked that his own people:

> ... hearing what gain the French and Fishermen made by
> trading of pieces, powder, and shot to the Indians ... began
> the practice of the same in these parts ... and made this
> thing common, notwithstanding any laws to the contrary.
> (Bradford 1952:206–07)

The above was written during a later period, but writing in the same
vein about the year 1628, Bradford bemoans that: "Those Indians ... which
had commerce with ye French got peeces of them and they in ye end made
a common trade of it." (Bradford 1952:286). This sentiment reappears in
William Wood's comments in 1634, where he refers to the Natives getting
"guns which they dayly trade for with the French, who will sell his eyes,
as they say, for a beaver."

In light of the evidence, not only regarding French attitudes and
policies on the gun trade, but also their incapacity to arm themselves, let
alone Natives with whom they had no alliance, these characterizations on
the part of the English seem somewhat unfair. However, Bradford's alarm-
ist tone may be explained in part by his need to generate increased English
support for the colony.

William Bradford was particularly nervous about the Indian gun
trade. Even though the settlers did not succeed in setting up their own
powder mill until 1676, he lived in fear that the Natives would learn the
secrets of gunpowder manufacture. Thus, when he wrote of the year 1628
he may have been unnecessarily pessimistic:

> ... [the Wampum trade] fills them with peeces, powder and
> shote ... by reason of ye baseness of sundry unworthy
> persons, both English, Dutch, and French which may turn
> to ye ruine of many. (Bradford 1952:286)

In fact, it would appear that this very year was the first occasion
when the Natives were provided with "peeces" by the Plymouth colony.
The culprit in this case was Thomas Morton, who taught some Indians how
to use arquebuses in order to hunt wildfowl. We can not be sure how many
guns passed into Native hands, nor whether the weapons were loaned or
traded. We do know how the English reacted.

Morton was seized by the people of Plymouth and Salem, and was
shipped back to England for punishment (Increase Mather 1972:21). This
swift sanction is indicative that the English probably countenanced few
violations of the arms trade prohibition at this time. It is probable that the
Royal Proclamation of 1622 forbidding the trade in weapons, and that of
1630 forbidding anyone to teach an Indian "to make or amend" firearms
"or anything belonging to them," was in concert with popular opinion

(Malone 1973:53, Bradford 1952:207). It is unlikely, however, that Morton traded more than a very small number of guns (Malone 1991:43).

It was not until 1639 that the fur trade in New Netherlands ceased to be a monopoly of the West India Company. Prior to this date, the Company's control of imports and exports, considerations of security, and the Company's legal authority over the settlers, seem to have effectively suppressed the gun trade (Trigger 1976:630, Trelease 1971:61, 95, 112–13).

1637 During Pequot War Until 1640

The earliest reference we have to the Dutch gun trade was in 1637, when the Pequot were observed to be in possession of a larger stock of firearms than their previous arsenal of two. The Dutch, according to Increase Mather (1972:53), had sold them some more. Captain Mason, who led both of the major massacres which resulted in the death or dispersal of the Pequot population, has left a detailed account of these encounters.

The Pequot, under their Sachem Sassacus, were the first New England tribe to recognize the threat which English colonization posed to their rights of land use and traditional ways of life. They attempted to ally with the Narragansett against the English. Sassacus argued that it would only be necessary to harass the invaders by burning their buildings and killing their cattle (Trumbull 1846:50). In May 1637, Captain (later Major) John Mason led a force of seventy-seven men from Connecticut and Massachusetts, which was joined by a contingent of Narragansetts and Mohegans. Mason attacked the Pequot at their fort on the Mistick River and massacred five to seven hundred individuals, who were armed only with bows and tomahawks (Mason 1967:19, Knowles 1934:132).

Bows appear to have been the only weapons used by the Pequot during the second and decisive battle of the war (Winthrop 1972, Mason 1967). While we are told that by 1637 the Pequot had little familiarity with gunpowder and dreaded it extremely (Thomson 1887:34), Captain Mason describes them as "munitioned well." It would appear that he was referring to other weapons besides firearms for he describes, in the same breath, the Pequot as "having sixteen guns with powder and shot" (Mason 1967:2), an estimate also cited by Mather (1972:28) and mistakenly attributed to Allyn. It would appear that not all of this arsenal was of Dutch origin: "he heard six guns, which persuaded him that the English were come, but drawing nearer he found they were the guns which formerly the Pequots got from the English." (Letter: Roger Williams to John Winthrop in Winthrop 1638–1644, M.H.S. 1944) It would seem then that the Dutch, like the English and French, were at most trading a few weapons illegally to the Indians. There are no references to the use of guns in battle by Natives, but there are many references to their use of arrows (for example, Mason 1967:9,11,19,22, Trumbull 1846:57, Mather 1972:45–46, 52–54, 57).

It was, however, during this period that the era of the weapons trade began. Champlain died and was succeeded by Governor Montmagny in June 1636. Montmagny permitted the sale of guns, at least to Christian converts. Then in 1639 the Dutch settlers became free to carry on trade independent of the Company. While the French allowed only limited gun-trade with the Indians, and the Dutch banned it altogether, the large potential profit motivated a great many colonists to ignore the law (Hyde 1962, Trigger 1976:630–31, 1985:204, Tooker 1963:117–18, Malone 1973:57, Mayer 1943:45). It seems most unlikely, however, that the colonists or other traders were in a position to deliver flintlock muskets in numbers sufficient to foster dependency or to pose a serious military threat to the colonies.

Chapter Five

The Weapons Trade Begins in Earnest

This chapter examines the historical record for evidence of the armaments used by the Iroquois and their Huron enemies between 1640 and 1648. More general evidence that the Iroquois' suppliers, the Dutch and English, were trading muskets to Indians prior to the Iroquois/Huron War of 1648–52 is also considered.

Most of the arms trade was illegal. This has led some scholars to argue that such trade was, in fact, far more extensive than official records suggest. Thus, it behooves us to examine our data sources closely. The reports which scholars use to support the theory of extensive weapons trade before 1650 were written by those for whom this speculation was a life or death matter. From Isaac Joques (1643) to Cotton Mather (1676), all of our informants were members of a population at risk, greatly outnumbered by Natives with whom they were clearly in competition. Naturally, the Europeans in this position were extremely sensitive to any hint of hostile Native activity. Thus, when the Pequot showed signs of unrest in 1637, the colonists coldly massacred them. The few survivors were hunted down with a fanaticism which only fear can engender (Mason 1967, Mather 1972). Similarly, when only five years later (1642) the colonists heard further reports of Native unrest, they adopted vigorous offensive measures. In Connecticut, for example, these took the form of a plan to attack the Natives before they could prepare for war. This attack was to take place without warning or provocation (Knowles 1934:190–192).

Again, when rumours spread that the Wampanoag were beginning to resent the continual invasion of their hunting territory, the reaction of the settlers seems extreme. In July 1662, Major Winslow seized his colony's ally Alexander, chief of the Wampanoag and son of Chief Massasoit, without whom the English would never have been able to survive in the New World (Hubbard 1974).

When the unarmed Sachem refused to be summoned like a servant rather than a king and ally, he was forced at gunpoint to do so (Hubbard 1974). Thus humiliated, Alexander was brought before the General Court. The chief protested that his friendship for the English was as firm as that of his father, and pointed out that the English were responding to rumours which were baseless. Recognizing this, the English fined Alexander for the trouble they had gone to, and released him. Shortly thereafter he died; some said of sheer frustration, others by English poison (Trumbull 1846). Similar absurdities were practised by the English after Alexander's brother Metacomet, whom they called Philip, inherited Sachemship. The English maltreatment of their allies eventually led to the disastrous King Philip's War of 1675–76.

In view of the extreme sensitivity of the colonists, which manifested itself in actions such as those outlined above (Jennings 1975), we must be sceptical when we examine their reports of Native psychological or material preparedness to attack them. We should also be wary of our informants' claims that colonists of other nationalities were primarily responsible for arming the Indians. All of the European colonies accused each other of trading arms to the Natives. All, at one time or another, prohibited such trade, and all engaged in it. The English accused the French and Dutch; the Dutch, the Swedes and English; the French, the English and Dutch, while the Swedes freely accused all of their colonial competitors and engaged in the trade.[1]

This chapter focuses closely on the period in which Native dependence upon personal firearms has been posited as a motivation for Iroquois warfare. We have seen in the previous chapter that prior to 1640, very few guns reached the Natives. However, as the next decade began two events, one in New France and one in New Holland, initiated the gun trade era for the Huron and Iroquois. First, Champlain, who rigorously opposed the sale of guns to any Indians, died and was replaced by Montmagny in June 1636. At the urging of the Jesuits, the new governor permitted the sale of muskets to Christian converts. Apparently their new role as weapons brokers to the Huron was useful to the Jesuits, for in 1643 Vimont reported

---

[1] For discussions of this colonial rivalry and mutual suspicion of participation in the gun trade to Natives see: Russell 1967, Mayer 1943, Snyderman 1948, Leach 1958, Burke 1967, Hubbard 1865, Tompson 1887, Trumbull 1846, Ellis and Morris 1906, Trelease 1960, Clark 1970, Douglas 1913, Malone 1973.

that: "The use of arquebusses, refused to the Infidels by Monsieur the Governor, and granted to the Christian Neophytes, is a powerful attraction to win them." (Thwaites 1896–1901:25:27) Second, in 1639 Dutch settlers were freed of the Company monopoly and could engage in the fur trade privately. This certainly made guns more available to the Iroquois, although the trade was still illegal. Where the French now permitted at least limited trade in firearms, the Dutch still forbade the sale of guns to Natives under penalty of death (Van Laer 1974:426). There is, however, a great deal of evidence to suggest that the huge profit to be derived from smuggling guns was enough to motivate many traders to ignore the law (Hyde 1962, Trigger 1976:630–1, Malone 1973:57, Mayer 1943:45).

These changes in the Dutch and French trade situations combined with the increasing availability of flint-guns ushered in the era of Indian gun trade, which began in the 1640s. We know that the gun trade was virtually non-existent prior to 1640. We also know that by 1675, a great many Indians possessed flint muskets (see Chapter Six for a discussion of Native arms after 1655). Having established a starting point for the gun trade and also a time at which the trade volume was significant, we must now attempt to narrow our focus to the shorter period between 1640 and the Iroquois victories over the Huron at the end of that decade.

There is little doubt that firearms sales to Natives increased enormously between 1640 and 1675. But was that increase as marked during the first few years of the first decade of trade as some authors suggest? In the next chapter I argue that as late as 1676 the gun was by no means the Indian's primary weapon. One might reasonably assume, in the absence of evidence to the contrary, that the increase in weapons trade between 1640 and this time was gradual.

Hunt and his followers, on the contrary, have argued that the products of European technology rapidly become extremely important to the Indians. In his *Wars of the Iroquois*, George Hunt suggested that Iroquois, especially Mohawk, dependence on European trade was sufficiently complete by 1640 that the inability to engage in this trade would have had disastrous consequences:

> The European trade instantly divided the tribes into highly competitive groups, and the competition for trade was, or soon became, a struggle for survival. The Native who had known and used the keen steel tools of the White man was unlikely to renounce them and was shortly unable to do so, so swiftly did the skills of the stone age vanish. (Hunt 1972:19)

Hunt's further comment, that a primary locus of Iroquois dependency was the European firearm, is more directly relevant to the present investigation. He suggests that the Iroquois were involved in an "arms race" which they could ill afford to lose. Hunt further believes that prior to 1648 the Iroquois required guns and ammunition to obtain food (1972:19, 35).

This torch is taken up by other scholars who add (as Hunt specifically does not) that the success of the Iroquois against the Huron and other tribes can be attributed to their access to firearms (Tooker 1963, Goldstein 1969): "[t]he Iroquois who were able to secure more guns than were their rivals, gradually gained the upper hand." (Tooker 1963). Trigger, in his classic work on the Huron, offers an alternate interpretation, suggesting that the "practical advantage of a cumbersome musket over a metal tipped arrow is doubtful." "The real power of the gun in Indian warfare appears to have been psychological; its noise and mysterious operation added to the terrors of foes and to the confidence of those who used them." (Trigger 1976:629) In his recent work *Natives and Newcomers* he cites Jennings:

> ... the thunderous noise they made and their ability to kill by injecting a metal charm into the body, or so the Indians believed, constituted supernatural properties that made them a source of terror to those who did not possess them. (Jennings 1984:80)

Trigger goes on to suggest that firearms had the additional effect that "They also increased the self-confidence of their owners." (Trigger 1985:262–3) Several questions arise at this point in our exploration:

- Did the Iroquois at this time acquire sufficient numbers of guns that they could have conferred some sort of military advantage, given that such an advantage was possible?
- Did the Iroquois actually obtain more guns than Natives allied with the French?
- Is there reason to believe that firearms, as they were deployed in Native warfare, were more efficacious in some way than aboriginal projectile weapons, or that they were perceived as such by the Indians?

The final question will be addressed in later chapters but I will speak to the first two issues here. We have very little hard documentary evidence (bills of lading, official invoices *etc.*) for this period, and especially few for the Dutch for the early 1640s. This is most unfortunate, for it is they who are usually deemed to have been the Mohawks' main supplier (Hyde 1962:120, Tooker 1963:117).

> The Mohawks . . . The settlement of the Dutch is near them; they go thither to carry on their trade, especially in arquebuses; . . . [the] Mohawks rob Hurons and Algonquins of their peltry which they go and trade to the Dutch for powder and arquebuses. (Thwaites 1896–1901: 24:271)

> . . . toward the end of the last century the Mohawks were reduced so low by the Algonquins that there seemed to be hardly any more of them on earth . . . But Mohawks reversed their bad fortune by the aid of Dutch firearms. Dutch came in thirty years ago. Firearms have rendered the Iroquois formidable over all their neighbours. (Thwaites 1896–1901:45:205)

There is little doubt that Dutch settlers did traffic illegally in weapons after 1639 (Hyde 1962:120, Mayer 1943:50, Trigger 1976:630–31, 1985:262) and we know that the Dutch sanctioned some trade in firearms after 1643 through a treaty with the Mohawk (Mayer 1943:49). Let us establish, as clearly as possible, the point in time at which large numbers of these weapons reached the Iroquois and other Natives trading with the Dutch and English.

Tooker and others expressly attribute Iroquois victories over the Huron to the large number of guns possessed by the former nation. These theorists must assume, then, that the Iroquois' enemies had relatively few firearms. While Champlain was alive, a rigid policy was maintained prohibiting the gun trade and prescribing the death penalty for offenders (Biggar 1922–36:5:3, Gooding 1962:25). This is hardly surprising in view of the state of Champlain's own arsenal (see Chapter Two). In fact, during this period no guns were traded to the Huron or Algonkian, who traded solely with the French (Trigger 1976:630). Weapons *were* traded out of Quebec after 1629 (again to the Montagnais) by the English during their brief occupation (Thwaites 1896–1901:6:309). It would seem that, realizing that their sojourn was temporary, they saw no reason to restrain themselves. Once the French were again in control they continued their prohibition of the gun trade. Sufficient numbers of guns were in use by now, however, that in 1634 Le Jeune was able to report that some of the Montagnais were good marksmen. The French deemed it expedient, while prohibiting the sale of guns, to sell limited quantities of powder and shot to those who already had them.

It would appear that, aside from the Montagnais' matchlocks, no significant number of firearms reached Natives within the French sphere of interest. In 1633, the Huron so little understood the weapons that they were still asking the French to shoot the Thunderbird from the sky in order to divert storms (Trigger 1976:431). Rather than arm them with arquebuses, the Jesuits promised the Attignawanton during 1635–36 that their hired men would defend their villages with guns. In addition, they supplied the Natives with iron arrowheads (Thwaites 1896–1901:10:53).

In the period between 1640 and the dispersal of the Huron, the French, influenced by the Jesuits, were restricting the sale of guns to only Huron Christian converts (Thwaites 1896–1901:25:27), thus placing the missionaries in the position of weapons brokers. By the year 1648, at least 120 Huron Christian traders were eligible to buy guns from the French (Thwaites 1896–1901:32:179). In addition, the Huron and their allies received some guns as gifts (for example, Thwaites 1896–1901:20:215). While his reports are not always the most reliable data source, Francis Gendron suggested that their military strength had declined because the Huron put too much faith in the arms that the French sold them at Quebec (Gendron 1868:17.[2] Nevertheless, from the scanty available data, it would appear that the Iroquois, or at least the Mohawk, did have more guns than the Huron, perhaps twice or even three times as many. However, the number of firearms possessed by either side was probably very small.

While much of the archaeological evidence from Huronia suffers from dating difficulties (Puype 1985:3), Kenneth Kidd's 1949 excavation of Ste. Marie I provides us with a window on Huron artifacts between 1639 and 1649, after which the site was abandoned and burned by the Jesuits who had founded it. Kidd's work revealed various fragments of barrels and gun parts. While no complete barrels, let alone complete guns, were found, "fragments of heavy iron tubes" with diameters between 7/8 and 1 3/4 in. were unearthed. Kidd believes that these "were almost certainly exploded gun barrels." Twelve objects were tentatively identified as parts of ramrods, and 2 were identified with certainty as ramrods. He also found 14 specimens which could have been gun springs of the period along with 33 objects which could have been parts of guns, "triggers, sears, flint-holders, and plates and mechanisms no longer used" along with seven pieces of lead shot (Kidd 1949:123–25). Kidd describes two specimens which almost certainly belonged to flint guns. One of these was brass-plated, while a cap associated with it was also brass plated and "finely engraved,"

[2] We must remember too, that the Iroquois had also to fight the Algonquin, who possessed guns by 1642 (Thwaites 1896–1901:24:23,57, 233). The Algonquins resident at Montreal Island had enough firearms by 1645 to fire an impressive salute (Thwaites 1896–1901:29:181).

possibly a presentation piece (for example, Thwaites 1896–1901:20:215). Kidd remarks (citing Greener 1986) that the presence of evidence of flint guns is "an interesting sidelight on the rapidity of diffusion, in that the flintlock seems to have been invented just prior to 1630 and was not readily adopted in France." The archaeological evidence from ten years of habitation of Ste. Marie I then, supports our conclusions from the archival evidence that relatively few guns were in the hands of the Huron by 1649 and that some of those guns were flintlocks.[3]

It would seem that the Mohawk got their first firearms from the English (Jameson 1959:274). This could explain why they ignored the Dutch and carried their furs to the English traders along the Connecticut River in 1640 (Van Laer 1974:483–4, Trigger 1976:631). Tooker suggests that the Mohawks' favourable trading position, which allowed them to play off English and Dutch against each other, gave them the buying power to acquire at a reasonable price goods which had become necessities, "especially guns" (Tooker 1963:116).

The Dutch, presumably, were convinced that in order to attract the Indian trade it would be necessary to equal English willingness to sell guns. In all likelihood, the English only dabbled in the arms trade, for they were more settlers than traders, and an armed Native population was more feared by them. It would appear that the Iroquois attempted unsuccessfully to convince the French to enter their "arms race," for in 1641 about 350 of them built two forts on the St. Lawrence as bases from which to negotiate. They asked the French for 30 muskets to add to the 36 they already had from the English and Dutch (Thwaites 1896–1901: 21:37). As far as we can tell, these few guns were all the Iroquois possessed before 1643.

The figure most often cited with regard to Iroquois armament is that of 400 muskets acquired from the Dutch by 1643 (Hyde 1962:120, Hunt

---

[3] Here I must disagree with Thomas Abler (1989:275) who acknowledges that relatively few remains of firearms were found in Huronia but, citing Kenneth Kidd (1949:125), tells us that "flintlocks were the only weapons [Kidd] recovered from the Jesuit mission of Sainte-Marie." Matchlocks also used springs and Kidd recovered "fourteen specimens . . . tentatively identified as springs, some of them gun springs . . . they would be clumsy yet powerful; yet similar ones may be seen on guns of the period." I am not confident that Kidd's evidence, even combined with Hunter's (1985:4) suggestion that some of these remains may be from snaphaunce weapons, argues for serious implementation of flint guns of any sort, let alone true flintlocks, at Ste-Marie I.

1972). This number echoes through the archival and ethnohistorical literature for some years:

1. The Jesuits tell us that by June 1643, the Mohawk had nearly 300 guns (Thwaites 1896–1901:24:271, 295).

2. The board of accounts in Holland reported that the Mohawk had guns and ammunition to supply 400 men, though sale to other Indians still was strictly forbidden (Jennings 1975:24,29). This trade was probably legitimized by Arent Van Curler's treaty between the Dutch and the Mohawk, negotiated in 1643, which preceded a further agreement of 1645 (O'Callaghan 1849:14–15).

3. In 1648 the English heard that the Narragansetts, who were close allies of the Mohawk (Knowles 1934:276) were preparing for war against the colonists. In August 1648, about 1,000 Indians were reported to have gathered in Connecticut with 300 guns among them. This group included "mercenary Mohawks [who] were said to be about 400 in number, all armed with guns and three pounds of powder for every man." (Mather 1972:66) After urgent diplomacy on the part of the English, "Wussoonkquassin gave peag to the Mohawks to retreat. It seems they are (Switzer-like) mercenary, and were hired on and off." (Roger Williams, letter dated Aug. 10, 1648) It would seem likely that John Winthrop was referring to these same Mohawk when he reports that in 1648 it was rumoured that the Narragansetts and Niantics had hired a number of outside Indians "about one thousand Indian Armed, three hundred or more having guns, powder and bullets." (Winthrop 1972:II:348, Ward 1961:127)

One might, of course, argue that the above figure of 300 to 400 Mohawk guns is merely the result of speculation by the European colonists. Nevertheless, the fact that Dutch, French and English sources refer to similar numbers of guns lends credence to the estimate. Apparently the Iroquois were able to buy guns legally until 1645, and probably illegally thereafter. *The Jesuit Relation* for this year suggests that Dutch firearms had enabled the Mohawk to become formidable over all their enemies (Thwaites 1896–1901:45:205).

Trigger (1969, 1976, 1985), Otterbein (1965) and Tooker (1963) rely on the assumption that a large volume of illegal trade permitted the Iroquois to build massive stocks of muskets by the time of their 1648 attack on

Huronia. In fact we have no reliable information after 1643 regarding the number of guns traded to these particular Indians. Some insight may, however, be gained from an examination of the colonists' gun-trade with Natives in general.

The authors who posit Iroquois dependency on European firearms as a motivational variable underlying trade-related warfare, base this assertion, in part, on more general assumptions. From the premise that such trade-dependency was virtually universal among Natives who had extensive contact with the Whites, Hunt (1972:18–19) and his followers (Quimby 1960, Goldstein 1969) deduce that the Iroquois were similarly addicted to European technology.

Having discussed the material which relates specifically to Iroquois and Huron arms, we will move on to discuss more general information concerning several other tribes which traded with the English and Dutch, and, to a lesser extent, the Swedes to the south and French to the north. If the Iroquois, or more accurately, the Mohawk, were acquiring guns in the quantities that some authors imply (Trigger 1976, 1985, Otterbein 1965, Tooker 1963), then it follows that other tribes with similar alliances would have been supplied in a similar manner.

The Narragansett, for example, had close ties with the Mohawk (Mather 1972:63,66, Roger Williams in Knowles 1934:341) and would surely have had access to the Dutch trade. The Mohegans were closely allied with the Mohawk and the British, and during most periods the Narragansett would also have had access to this source of goods. The Niantic and others were allied with the Narragansett. The Minqual were able to trade with both the Dutch and Swedes (O'Callaghan 1849). It would seem however, that the Mohawk were the only tribe to use guns during this period, perhaps because they prized them whereas most other tribes had a low opinion of the weapons (Hyde 1962:120).

The Eries had few guns, and were reported to prefer the bow, perhaps with poison arrows (Hyde 1962:125). When the Narragansett prepared for war with the Mohegans around 1648, the New England colonists were disturbed to hear that they had brought in Mohawk who had guns (Winthrop 1972:II:348, Ward 1961:127, Knowles 1934:218–220). By 1657, it is reported that the Sioux had never seen a gun (Hyde 1962:133). In fact the Siouan-speaking peoples who lived west of Lake Superior did not have iron weapons of any sort (Trigger 1985:191). The Neutrals too, as of 1647, had no guns (Trigger 1976:736).

Rumours that Natives were beginning to learn the use of firearms circulated in New England as early as 1642 (Knowles 1934:190). The Commissioners of the United Colonies responded in 1644 by passing an act forbidding any person to sell any kind of arms or ammunition to an

Indian or to repair any weapon for him, and levying a heavy penalty for doing so. This measure was deemed necessary due to the rapid progress of the Indian in the use of firearms (Knowles 1934:203, Malone 1973:57). This trade was also forbidden at New Amsterdam under penalty of death and at Rensselaerwyck under pain of a 100-guilder fine and deportation (Van Laer 1974:565).

No guns were in evidence in 1643 when the Narragansetts, with 1,000 warriors under Miantinomo, fought the Mohegan under their English ally Uncas. It is noteworthy that the reason Uncas' men were able to apprehend Miantinomo was that the latter was wearing heavy armour and was unable to flee (Winthrop 1972:II:157, Ward 1961:120, Knowles 1934:192).

During the first years of this decade, the Dutch governor Kieft, through almost creative ineptness, brought about a series of hostilities between the Dutch and Natives. The most disastrous incident was in 1640 when incensed Algonquins massacred New Amsterdam colonists in what seems to have been a local episode (Mayer 1943:44). The colonists blamed the Dutch at Rensselaerwyck who were "organized under an independent charter not delegated to the West India Co. at Fort Amsterdam, especially in the matter of the sale of firearms." (Ruttenbur 1971:66–67) According to the "Report of the Board of Accounts on New Netherlands" for 1644, "Rensselaer's Colonie, lying on the North River in the neighbourhood of Fort Orange . . . experienced no trouble and enjoyed peace, because they continued to sell firearms and powder to the Indians even during the war against our people." (In Mayer 1943:45) We do not know if this trade was extensive, but can gain some understanding of the mood of the colonists from their reaction to these skirmishes. The "Report" continues to suggest: "that to restore peace and quiet throughout the land, the Indians who had waged war against us should be wholly destroyed and exterminated." To accomplish this end, the Director demanded 150 soldiers "armed with muskets and coates of maile." (Mayer 1943:46)

It was also in 1643 that Arent van Curler negotiated the treaty between the Dutch and Mohawk (O'Callaghan 1849:14–15) which legitimized the sale of a large number of guns to the latter. Sale of guns to other Natives was strictly forbidden (Tooker 1963:117–18, Jennings 1975:24–29, Trigger 1976:631, 1985:262). Some guns were in evidence among the Narragansett and their neighbours by 1646: "[At Waranoke] vaunting their arms, bows and arrows, hatchets and swords, some with their guns ready charged, before and in the presence of the English messengers they primed and cockt them ready to give fire." (Increase Mather 1972:63)

The above comments may indicate that these Natives had flint guns as early as 1646 (although one did have to prime and cock a matchlock). It is also possible that Mather, writing at a time when flintlocks were the norm, and matchlocks banned (Russell 1957:10), about events in which he had taken no part personally, may have simply embellished his account without regard to the historical accuracy of these details.

It is quite possible that the guns at Waranoke were in the hands of the Narragansett's old allies the Mohawks, for in 1648 we hear that as the Narragansett prepared for war they were joined by "the mercenary Mohawks [who] were said to be about 400 in number, all armed with guns and three pound of powder for every man." (Increase Mather 1972:66)

Little evidence exists that the Narragansett had guns of their own before 1660. Indeed, the English were alarmed in 1653 when their ally Uncas informed them that Ninnigret, a Narragansett Sachem, had been to "Manhatos" and had given the Dutch governor a "great present of Wampum and received from him twenty guns with powder and shot answerable." (Increase Mather 1972:67)

Few Indians other than the Mohawk seem to have had firearms in the 1640s. In 1647 the Raritans, accustomed to Dutch trade, attacked the Dutch yacht *De Vreede*. Van der Bogart in his report of the incident (on July 17 of that year) testified that the Indians "came on board in large numbers, all armed with tomahawks, rapier blades and other weapons." (van der Bogart 17/6/1647 in Van Laer 1974:157,409)

No colonial government was anxious to sell large quantities of guns to the Indians, but the Dutch has some special problems. In 1643, as we have seen, the sale of guns to the Mohawk was necessary in order to establish good relations with this tribe. According to Dutch estimates, the sales permitted about 400 to reach these Indians by 1644 (Trigger 1976:631, 1985:262). Other sources indicate 300 guns in use by 1643 (Thwaites 1896–1901:271,295, Ward 1961:127).

In 1643, some of the Mohawk supplied guns to the Mohegan, who fought with New Netherlands for two years (Russell 1957:13). As mentioned earlier, they spared the Rensselaerwyck colony which was a supplier of guns (Mayer 1943:51–52). In 1645, French protest led again to a ban on sales to Indians, but fear that the Natives might destroy the weak Dutch colony if the trade was denied them led the directors in Amsterdam to permit the regulated sale of small numbers of guns by Company officials, although sale by private traders remained illegal (O'Callaghan 1849:14:83). There is evidence that the Dutch did enforce the ban on private trade in arquebuses. In 1648, Governor Stuyvesant charged two traders at Fort Orange with violating the ban (Trigger 1976:631). The same year, some freemen and sailors on the ships *Valckenier* and *Pynappel*, arriving from Europe, were found to have "a few snaphaunce" and these were confiscated. These individuals claimed that they had brought the guns for their personal defence, but as they did not have import certificates from the

Chamber at Amsterdam, the weapons were subject to confiscation. The next year "one Gerrit Vastrick, a trader, was authorized to bring with him a case of guns, as is ascertained, in order, as it was reported, to supply the Indians with a sparing hand." (Jameson 1959). Secretary Van Tienhoven, presenting the position of the Council of Colony Rensselaerwyck, says in contradiction to the Council for the Communality that the thirty guns (one case) imported by Vastrick were to be sold to Dutch colonists who were without firearms (Van Tienhoven 1649 in Mayer 1943:50–51).

As might be expected, the policy of selling guns officially to the Indians while prohibiting private trade resulted in an outcry from the Dutch traders who could buy a gun for eight guilders (or one beaver) in Amsterdam (Mayer 1943:49) and sell it to the Indians for as much as twenty times that amount (Jameson 1959). The Council for the Commonality laid a charge against Director Stuyvesant, who condemned the gun trade yet engaged in it himself. To a remonstrance of 1649 to the home government regarding "The Administration of Director Stuyvesant," the Directors of the West India Company replied in a lengthy justification dated January 27, 1650: "The Directors in Amsterdam have given orders to Stuyvesant to sell articles of contraband, such as guns, powder, and lead, to the Indians." (Mayer 1943:49) Their reasons are best expressed by Secretary van Tienhoven, writing in defence of Stuyvesant in 1649. He argues that on his arrival, he (Stuyvesant) quietly tried to end the trade in guns and ammunition, but was petitioned by the colony Rensselaerwyck for moderation. Wholesale warfare against the colonists would result if trade was wholly abolished. Therefore, the Director and Council:

> . . . resolved to barter sparingly a few guns and a little powder through the Commissary at Fort Orange on the Company's account; taking good care, moreover, that the sloops navigating the river should not convey any quantity up . . . 'Tis to be observed in this place, that the Director dreading one of two evils, permitted some arms to be bartered in the Fort in order to preserve the colonie from danger . . . the seizure of some guns by leave of the Director, happened because they were not accompanied by any permit, as ordered by the Company. Under such guize many guns could be introduced. (Van Tienhoven 1649 in Mayer 1943:50)

The Company's reasons for engaging in this trade were not purely altruistic. On March 7, 1650 these "Observations On the Duties Seized on Goods to New Netherlands" stated:

As the greatest profit arised from powder, lead, guns and similar articles, the sale of which to the Indians being contraband is prohibited on pain of corporal punishment, yet as the gain derived therefrom is stimulating, and as a small capital is always realized, through these and such finesses, by people of small means, the country is overrun with them. The yearly amount is considerable from which the Company derives no duties, the transaction being concealed from government in New Netherlands in the year 1649, the Company permitted the Director to supply the Indians sparingly with powder, lead, and guns. (Mayer 1943:51)

Enough of an outcry was raised by the New World Dutch that in 1650 the "Committee of the States General" in its "Report On the Affairs of New Netherlands" felt obliged to reaffirm the prohibition of illicit trade and the punishment for violations:

. . . especially for what occurred during the war, when subjects of this state dared to strengthen their enemies by the sale of prohibited articles of contraband. And whereas this evil has now reached that stage that the trade in the aforesaid contraband goods cannot easily be cut short or forbidden without evident danger of new war and trouble between the subjects of this State and the Aborigines, the Council of New Netherlands shall be notified and ordered to take care that none of the aforesaid articles contraband shall be hereafter traded and sold by colonists, or other inhabitants, except with its knowledge and by its order . . .

And here the Committee gets itself in trouble:

. . . the guns to be charged at six guilders, the pistols at four guilders, the pound of powder at six stivers, all for the benefit of the public interests there; so as in time, when it can, in their opinion, be safely done, to forbid trade altogether, under heavy penalties to be thereunto enacted. (in Mayer 1943: 51–52)

Only six guilders for a gun! The Indians would gladly pay many times that amount. As Chambers, writing in 1650, observed: "This small charge is wholly unnecessary inasmuch as the Indians will readily purchase guns in the Spring [at] 120 guilders and a pound of powder at 10 or 12 guilders." (Chambers in Mayer 1943:52)

It is possible that these Company policies resulted in an increase in the volume of guns being traded. Most authors have assumed that wholesale trade in weapons was the norm, regardless of Company rules and law, (for example, Trigger 1976, Tooker 1963, Otterbein 1965, Russell 1957). There is, however, some support for the contention that the law was effectively enforced. Firstly, it is a matter of record that ships arriving at New Netherlands were inspected, and contraband goods seized (Mayer 1943:50). Smuggling did occur. For example, in 1653 at New Haven some Dutchmen were apprehended for having concealed gun barrels and locks inside liquor casks (Malone 1973:57). With Dutch authorities becoming increasingly sensitive, the volume of such importation must necessarily have been quite limited. Secondly, after the Company began to sell guns in 1649, there was a noticeable increase in the numbers of local Natives who possessed them, much to the consternation of the colonists (Mayer 1943:53).

The authorities were so successful in controlling the importation of guns that the Seneca were obliged to approach the Governor with a request for permission to buy some. Their argument is the same as that often cited as the primary Dutch motive for arming the enemies of the Huron: "We have a vast deal of trouble collecting beavers through the enemy country. We ask to be furnished with powder and ball. If our enemies conquer us, where will ye then obtain beavers?" (Mayer 1943:54) Stuyvesant responded by giving them a single keg of powder and entreating them to make peace with the Minsi so that the Dutch might "use the road to them in safety." (Mayer 1943)

It would appear that the Mohawk and Huron were the only tribes to acquire a significant number of guns prior to the 1650s, and even they received relatively few weapons.

During the second half of this century the weapons trade began to escalate, as Natives increasingly began to value the firearm. A ready explanation for this may be found in the greater availability of flint guns, a weapon suited to Indian-style "flying warfare." (K.P. in Lincoln 1966) Because they feared the military potential of flintlock guns in Native hands, the Dutch enacted a regulation in 1656 which forbade new colonists to bring with them other than matchlock weapons. By 1664, when the English conquered New Netherlands, none of the European colonies considered the matchlock an acceptable weapon and all were equipping themselves with flint guns (Russell 1957:10), either snaphaunce of true flintlock as well as matchlocks.

As usual, the Natives tried to play off sources of supply against each other. For example, the Minquas Chiefs Aguarcochquo and Quadicko informed the Dutch on July 13, 1647 that the Swedish Governor resident at the South River of New Netherlands had said that he could sell them ample supplies of powder, lead, and guns but that the Dutch, being poor, could not do so (O'Callaghan 1849:II:158). In 1653, nine Sagamores who lived near Manhatos felt obliged to inform the English that the "Dutch had solicited them by promising them gunns, swords, powder, wampum, waist coats, and coats to cut off the English . . ." (Increase Mather 1972:68) Similarly, when seven Huron and Ottawas arrived in three canoes at Trois Rivières in 1653, they said that their groups would arrive next year with many beaver to trade for guns and ammunition in order to make themselves more formidable to their enemies (Thwaites 1896–1901:40:213–15), implying that their ability to fight the Iroquois would benefit the French. Seneca's argument to the Dutch, that his people would be unable to obtain beaver for lack of firearms (above, Mayer 1943:54) carried the same implication.

There is little evidence to suggest that their pleas, or those of any of the tribes, were answered with large numbers of firearms prior to the destruction of Huronia. The archaeological evidence certainly supports my suggestion that Natives were very particular about the types of firearm they would purchase. Bradley tells us that parts recovered from the Onondaga sites were "first-class quality flintlocks." (Bradley 1987:142) He lists gun parts from three sites as follows:

> Shurtleff site: five parts including one lockplate, two pieces of barrel, one verticle sear, one sheet brass, and one buttplate, one European gunflint and two Native made gunflints. Two European sword blades were also found.

The Shurtleff site was probably occupied from 1630 until 1640 (Bradley 1987:116) and is the earliest site at which firearms artifacts have been found. The verticle sear, lockplate and flint are indicative of the use of flint guns of one sort or another. Not surprisingly, given the dates of likely occupation, there is little evidence of serious implementation of firearms.

> Carley site: eleven parts including one complete lock, a snaphaunce cock, a pistol cock, a trigger and a lock plate screw along with miscellaneous fittings and furniture and one European gunflint.

The Carley site artifacts cover the period from 1640 to 1650 (Bradley 1987:116). The complete lock, snaphaunce cock, pistol cock and gunflint are specific to flint weapons.

> Lot 18: fifty-three parts including two musket cocks, two pistol cocks, five batterys, four top jaws, six pans, six springs, three triggers, one sear, one tumbler and six lock-

plate screws as well as miscellaneous fittings and furniture. (Bradley 1987:143)

Lot 18's probable dates are 1650–55 (Bradley 1987:116). At this later period we find much more evidence of firearm use in general and, additionally, of the employment of flint guns. Of these artifacts, the cocks, "batterys," top jaws, pans, sear and tumbler are clearly from flint guns.

Charles Wray's (1985)[4] work on the Seneca uncovered further archaeological evidence that the Iroquois were particular about the kinds of firearms for which they would trade. Almost all of the gun parts were from flint guns although evidence for relatively few firearms was found. Of the 210 excavated burials at the Powerhouse site (RMSC/Wray Site No. 24, probably occupied between 1635 and 1655), only 13 yielded guns or gun parts. Ten complete locks were found, along with 11 batterys, 11 lock screws, 5 breech plugs, 4 butt plates, 11 upper cock jaws, 13 cocks, 8 pans, 5 battery and sear springs, 12 main springs, 12 triggers, 5 trigger-guards, 16 tumblers, 1 matchlock serpentine (may also be referred to as a cock) and 100 lead balls. Puype (1985:75) classifies the 15 locks or lock plates (the shape of which is central to his excellent taxonomy of lock types) as follows:

- One Type 1 lock plate with an English lock mechanism (1630–50);
- Six Type 2 locks or lock plates (1625–55) one of which (No. 6242/24) is clearly a snaphaunce, not a true flintlock;
- Four Type 4 artifacts (1635–50);
- Three Type 5 lockplates, one Type "A" (1650–65), one Type "B" (1655–after 1660), One Type "C" (1655–70);
- One Type 6 lock plate (*circa* 1655).

Peter Pratt, in his *Archaeology of the Oneida Iroquois* tells us that the Thurston site (probably 1630 to before 1650, see Pratt 1976:137) provides the earliest evidence of firearms in Oneida territory: "two lead pellets were found in the refuse." The Marshall site, which Thurston antedates, yielded one lead pellet in a burial and three in refuse (Pratt 1976:143).

There is evidence then of the presence of flint guns, though not necessarily true flintlocks, but little evidence of serious implementation by the time of the Iroquois wars.

[4]Paper given at the Trade Gun Conference, Rochester Museum and Science Centre, Rochester N.Y., June 9, 1984 (cited by Puype 1985:75).

European Weapons and Native Tactics

To suggest that one side or another may have had more guns is not necessarily to disagree with Snyderman (1948:56), who states that the warfare practices of the Iroquois were virtually identical with those of their neighbours. Nor does such a stance imply disagreement with Raymond Scheele: "The instruments and weapons of war used by all tribes were similar . . . Actual fighting tactics were the same for all tribes." (Scheele 1950:83–84) The suggestion by some authors (for example, Trigger 1976, Otterbein 1965) that the use of firearms occasioned changes in Native tactics is predicated on the assumption that the weapons were widely used, and that they were significant enough in their impact to require adaptation.

Bruce Trigger (1976) suggests that Iroquois tactics began to adapt to deal with the new weapons within a year of the Iroquois' first encounter with them. He believes that by the time of their second encounter with European arquebuses, June 19, 1610, the Mohawk had learned to drop to the ground to avoid being hit. He remarks that Lescarbot observed that Indians in the southeastern United States also learned to drop to the ground when shot at. Otterbein expands this notion somewhat further, suggesting that by 1647 the Huron too had developed this technique (Otterbein 1965). Such discussions of changing Native tactics appear to assume that their appropriateness would not have been obvious to any Indian and, further, that they were a specific adaptation to the gun. We are, after all, discussing Native persons having "learned" to duck in response to a launched projectile! The Mohegan, for example, employed the same defense against Narragansett arrows at the battle of Sachem's Plains (Trumbull 1846:60). Perhaps it is reasonable to suggest that once the Natives discovered that something other than noise and smoke came out the gun's barrel they employed strategies which had worked well with other projectile weapons.

In his stimulating paper "Why the Iroquois Won — An Analysis of Military Tactics" Keith Otterbein (1965) has incorporated Hunt's (1972) and other scholars' assumptions regarding Iroquois weapons superiority within the context of a general theory of the relationship between weapons and tactics.

Otterbein begins with the assertion that what the Indians really wanted to do was fight pitched, open-field battles (European style) by forming two lines in the open and discharging arrows at each other. He goes on to suggest that "Champlain put an end to these tactics when he introduced the matchlock to the Algonquins in 1609." Otterbein says that the Algonquins, thus armed, gained confidence to increase their attacks on the Iroquois. In the face of matchlock fire the Mohawk would retreat, and thus draw the Algonquins into ambushes. According to Otterbein: "tactics consisted in rushing upon the enemy and engaging in hand-to-hand combat before the Algonquins could do much damage with their matchlocks and bows and arrows." (Otterbein 1965:57–58)

Presumably because the Iroquois shields and bows were unequal to the Algonquin armament, they were not used in the charge. In these attacks the Mohawk discarded their shields, but not their armour; thrusting spears and war clubs replaced bows and arrows. The enemy "were probably still wearing body armour and would perhaps have chosen to fight in a battle line if possible." Otterbein goes on to say that these tactics were successful, and that the Iroquois "were able to maintain control of their hunting area through what is today known as guerrilla warfare." Because his theory is predicated on the assumption of firearms' efficacy, he continues: "Wiping out enemy raiding parties was undoubtedly a means of obtaining needed weapons." (Otterbein 1965:58, citing Wood [1634])

Citing Hunt (1972:167), Otterbein suggests that the Iroquois began by 1641 to obtain limited quantities of flint guns from the Dutch. He suggests that these weapons were suited to the Iroquois' new tactics: they would charge the enemy battle line, fire their weapons, and "fall upon the fleeing enemy who had been dislodged from their position by the onslaught." According to this author, the Huron had by 1647 developed a tactic for coping with these attacks.

> The Huron warriors would form a crescent; just before the Iroquois would fire their guns, the Hurons would drop to the ground; after the Iroquois had discharged their weapons, they would rise, fire their own guns, and counter charge the enemy.

Otterbein goes on to suggest that the "extensive use of firearms resulted in the abandonment of body armour . . . Armour was useless against bullets," and further, that "if men were close together, one discharge of a musket loaded with several balls could kill more than one warrior." (Otterbein 1965:58–59) This latter comment purports to account for the scattered deployment of warriors in this period.

Because Otterbein's analysis presents perhaps the most sophisticated model of the impact of the introduction of European guns to the Natives, it will be useful to examine it at some length. Our understanding of Otterbein's paper will be augmented if we consider his reason for writing it. He tells us in his conclusion (1965:61) that his analysis has "demonstrated the feasibility of using concepts, variables, and theories derived from the analysis of Western military history, for an understanding of the military success of a so-called primitive people."

Otterbein, quite reasonably, is trying to fit inter-tribal warfare into a model of tactical evolution developed by Tom Wintringham in his seminal work *The Story of Weapons and Tactics* (1943). In this study of the evolution of European warfare from ancient times to the present, Wintringham suggests that one may conceptualize changes in battle tactics in terms of three main variables. He posits that tactical change resulted from improvement in the effectiveness of (1) weaponry, or (2) armour, or from changes in (3) the mobility of armies. For example, where state-of-the-art weapons could not penetrate defensive armour, combatants emphasized armour technology as exemplified by the heavily armoured knight in medieval European siege-style warfare. When weapons were developed against which armour was not proof the emphasis shifted to mobility: defensive measures were abandoned or de-emphasized. For example, the introduction of the longbow which could penetrate armour led initially to an intense effort to improve that armour. Due to the firepower of the bow, this resulted in absurdly heavy and unmanageable contraptions which, as one author of the day wryly commented, at least prevented the knight from doing any harm to himself or others (Hughes 1974). The emphasis gradually shifted to mobility and armour was dropped altogether.

The side with the most effective weapons would be the victor, until more effective armour was available, or tactics based on high mobility were developed. Otterbein says he is using Wintringham's analysis of armour/weapons oscillation in studying the Iroquois "because it provides a means of determining which side had tactical superiority at a given time." (Otterbein 1965:57)

Otterbein suggests that the first period, when Iroquois used guerrilla warfare and hand-weapons against the Algonquin, was an "armoured phase," presumably because they were still wearing their reed body-armour (as was the enemy). The second period, after the Iroquois began to acquire firearms, is to him, "a transitional phase," while the third period, after 1660 when "nearly every Iroquois warrior had a musket," is posited as an "unarmored" or weapons predominant phase (Otterbein 1965:60–61).

While I admire his application of Wintringham's model, I think that the assumptions upon which his ethnohistorical case study are predicated may be fruitfully examined from a different perspective. I will start from the initial suggestion that the Natives preferred European-style pitched battles, but abandoned that tactic when guns were introduced.

The suggestion that aboriginal warfare consisted in the two sides forming two lines in the open and discharging arrows at each other may be incorrect. Champlain's frustration in 1615 with his Native allies was due to the fact that they refused to "stand," preferring instead to charge the enemy with warclubs and the like (Biggar 1922–36:3:67). At his second encounter with the Mohawk on June 19, 1610, Champlain and his company nearly exhausted their ammunition with little effect. They eventually resorted to war clubs and swords and stormed the fort (Trigger 1976:258). The only time when the Mohawk and Huron are known to have faced each other in the open was in 1609 when Champlain introduced them to the arquebus. I suspect that under normal circumstances this battle would have followed the progression typical of Native warfare: an initial volley of projectiles followed by hand-to-hand combat (Biggar 1922–36:3:67, Chown 1976–77, Kinetz 1965).

There is little support for the contention that the Iroquois were obtaining flint guns from the Dutch by 1641. Otterbein cites only Hunt (1972), who was careful to point out that the only large quantity of guns known to have reached the Iroquois was in their hands by 1643. Hunt also argues that the Iroquois probably did not have numerical superiority in weapons.

It is likely that a large proportion of the guns sold to Natives during this early period were matchlocks. As is shown in the previous chapter, the Dutch were in possession of few flint guns and valued these highly. It is improbable that they would provide potential enemies with weapons superior to their own. More likely, most flint guns were retained for colonial use, while those they replaced were made available to the Natives. Hagerty (1985:85) suggests that the presence of certain types of wheelocks "on an Indian site obviously shows that inefficient and unwanted pieces were traded to the Natives to get rid of them" while Bradley emphasizes the "first-class" quality of flint guns found at Onondaga Iroquois sites. Puype's archaeological evidence supports Bradley with regard to the types of firearms obtained by the Iroquois. Bradley observes that most of the locks from sites "with an estimated period of occupation ranging from 1630 to 1655 belong to the flintlock system." Both authors, I think, are correct. There is plenty of evidence that the Iroquois were quite discriminating with regard to the guns they wanted, but the historical evidence presented herein as well as the archaeological evidence from the Carley and Shurtleff sites discussed earlier, indicates that it is unlikely that they were able to obtain quantities of quality flintlocks in time to become dependent upon them as *casus belli* for the destruction of Huronia.

Otterbein suggests that the extensive use of firearms led to the abandonment of body armour because that armour was useless against bullets. This is certainly a plausible suggestion, in that armour was eventually abandoned. I would argue, however, that armour was abandoned not solely because it could not stand up to gunfire, but because it was little proof against metal-tipped arrows as well.[5] The need for mobility became readily apparent as the settlers gained experience in Native-style "guerrilla" warfare. This resulted in the colonists abandoning armour long before the Natives acquired guns (Peterson 1956, Malone 1973).

Regarding the notion that the use of multiple shot led to an attempt to spread out the battle line, my own testing would suggest that the two practices are unconnected. Four balls fired from a 0.65 bore musket with a very short barrel (24 inches — more of a blunderbuss than a musket) strike within 4 in. of each other at 25 yards and within 15 in. at 50 yards. Due to their relative inability to form an effective gas-seal, even at 50 yards the lethality of these projectiles is doubtful. Thus, it would seem that at any distance where a "brace of bullets" might be lethal, their spread is insufficient to significantly increase the chance of hitting a single target let alone one or two. For example, when Metacomet (King Philip) was shot in 1676, one of the bullets struck his heart and the other hit only 2 in. above it (Church 1772:123). It seems unlikely then that any group which had experience with the use of multiple-shot charges would see their use by other groups as a reason to change their battle strategy.

Otterbein suggests that the major use of arquebuses by the Iroquois was in attacking trade canoes from river banks (1965:59). He appears to feel that the guns would have been able to sink canoes more efficiently than bows and arrows. Firstly, I would argue that the Iroquois' object in attack was to acquire the peltry, rather than sink it. Secondly, it seems much more likely that one would be able to capsize a canoe by disturbing its occupants than to sink it by punching small holes in it. Thirdly, we return to the aforementioned problem of rate of fire. Even the most heavily laden canoe can be paddled out of range of gun or bow (no more than 100 yd) within one minute. During that time 10 musketeers can fire on average 10 shots. I have commented on the accuracy of the musket in Chapter Four. Let us

---

[5] If the Iroquois' enemy had no matchlocks, we are left either with no change in tactics, or need another theory to account for one. Bruce Trigger suggests a much more supportable hypothesis as to why Native tactics might have changed. He has argued that the use of iron arrowheads may have greatly reduced the effectiveness of Native armour (Trigger 1976:360,417). Whether soft iron represented much improvement over brass arrowheads already in use (Bradford and Winslow 1622:52,55) is difficult to say and, in light of Pope's research on the effectiveness of chert points (Pope 1918), even more so. Europeans, beginning with the Spanish during the 1500s, found that their armour was not proof against Native arrows with stone heads.

say, for now, that the chance of 50 percent, that is to say, 5 shots, hitting either canoe or occupants (at any range beyond that at which a large rock would be a more efficacious projectile), is not great. During this same period of time, the same attackers could easily fire 50 aimed broadhead arrows. Even if we allow no greater accuracy for the bow, we still have 25 iron arrowheads lodged in the hapless targets. If we add to this the fact that the bowman is free to chase his target along the riverbank much more easily than the arquebusier who has to reload, and further, that bows rarely misfire and never blow-up, an argument in favour of European weapons is difficult to support. Add to this the high cost of arquebuses, powder and lead, the frequency and inaccessibility of repairs, the weight of the weapon and accoutrements, the warning its report gives the enemy, and we must wonder why they bothered with guns at all. My explanation will be offered later in this work (Chapter Eight).

Although the Algonquins did not have a number of guns, and would have derived little advantage from them if they had (see Trigger 1976:630, Fisher 1977:16–17), further discussion about their impact may be instructive. Otterbein mentions that the dissected Allegheny Plateau and the Adirondack Mountains of upper New York State "are ideally suited for hiding war parties and staging ambushes." (1965:58) Unfortunately, this terrain is also unsuited to European-style, battle-line warfare, whether the combatants are armed with guns or bows and arrows.

The fire-in-ranks, open-field style battle is perhaps the only situation where the matchlock gun is of any use (see Chapter Two and also Schlesier 1975). This is evidenced by the persistence of rank-fire discipline in European warfare for over two hundred years beyond the scope of this study (Hughes 1974). If we are basing our model on European data as does Otterbein, how can we then suggest that the introduction of the gun led to abandonment of European-style firearms-oriented tactics?

Otterbein argues that the Natives abandoned their shields, but not their armour, using clubs and thrusting spears. He suggests that they left their bows behind and engaged in "hand to hand combat before the Algonquins could do much damage with their matchlocks and bows and arrows." (Otterbein 1965:58) In the style of warfare conjectured by Otterbein, mobility and tactics would be the key to victory, and suggest a stage that Wintringham (1943) would call a "transitional" rather than an "armoured phase."

Otterbein assumes that a great many firearms were present, at first in the hands of the Algonquins, and later in those of the Iroquois. He further assumes that these weapons were sufficiently superior to the Native bow that tactics designed to deal with the latter weapon were no longer adequate. Otterbein uses various incidents to support his theory that new tactics must have evolved in response to the use of guns. For example, citing a single incident as evidence for this trend, Otterbein suggests that the Iroquois began to lure the Algonquin into ambush by first pretending to flee and then rushing upon them, thus preventing the use of their superior firepower (Otterbein 1965:58, see quote at page 73–74).

Assuming that the Iroquois had acquired flint guns by 1641, Otterbein goes on to suggest that they and their Huron enemies developed tactics which were designed to defend against, and to deploy the gun effectively (Otterbein 1965:59). The Huron, according to this author, would duck down while the Iroquois obligingly discharged their weapons at empty space. Then the Huron would bob up *en masse*, and shoot at their attackers. Again, Otterbein bases speculation about broad changes in tactics on a single incident (Trigger 1976:754).

While it is quite probable that the incidents on which Otterbein's speculations are based did occur, he does not present adequate evidence that these were consistent with a change in general patterns of behaviour. Firstly, in order for either the earlier or later techniques to be effective repeatedly, we must envisage a high level of co-operation on the part of the enemy. Secondly, it is clear that even after they acquired large numbers of flint guns, Native people who fought in New England (including the Mohawk) fought individualistically, using what we now call guerrilla tactics. Thirdly, I again point to the probability that neither the Iroquois nor their enemies had enough guns prior to 1650 for guns to have had any substantial effect on Indian fighting-style. Evidence for extensive weapons trade cannot be found, and there are strong indications that the colonists had few guns to trade. Further, there is little reason to accept Otterbein's *a priori* assumption that a charge using a volley of arrows to dislodge the enemy would be less effective than such an attack involving firearms (see Chapter Seven). If tactical changes occurred by 1650 they were probably in response to several changes in the demand characteristics of warfare for Natives. The European use of artillery and highly developed fortifications, as well as their ignorance of the rules of traditional Native warfare, would require tactical adaptation in response. There is little reason to think that major changes in Native tactics resulted from the introduction of a single weapon.

The trade in muskets to Native people did not get its start until after 1640. Because the colonists had few flint guns for their own use, it is probable that most guns traded during this decade were matchlocks. The Huron and their allies were probably not seriously outgunned by the Iroquois as they too had access to a limited number of firearms. Otterbein's theory that Natives developed fighting tactics to incorporate firearms use is based on the unsupportable premise that a large-volume gun trade existed. The tactics which Otterbein and others present as adaptation to the presence of muskets on Native battlefields would have been equally useful where bows and arrows were used.

Hunt (1972), Tooker (1963), Otterbein (1965), Goldstein (1969) and many other scholars have assumed that the European arquebus of the seventeenth century was a vastly superior weapon to the Native self-bow. Trigger (1985:262–63) emphasizes the weapons' ability to inspire terror. If either hypothesis were correct, then the small numbers of firearms which the Iroquois were able to obtain might have given them the advantage in warfare. In Chapter Seven we will see whether in fact the musket's performance justifies the high opinion in which it is held by these authors. We have some reason to believe that three or four hundred muskets had reached the Mohawk by 1643, although even these estimates were speculation on the part of the French, Dutch and English. The illegal gun trade flourished no doubt, but probably did not involve substantial numbers of weapons.

Chapter Six

1655 to the End of King Philip's War 1676

Because of the difficulty in establishing with certainty the scope of the gun trade prior to the Iroquois wars we will also examine a later period. Logically, if Native tribes in close contact with Europeans did not have large numbers of guns after the Iroquois wars we might deduce that they did not have them during that earlier period. Here we examine the period between 1655 and King Philip's War in 1675–76 and explore evidence for the extensive use of muskets by Indian trading partners of the English and Dutch during this quarter century after the dispersal of the Huron. If, by the 1640s, the gun had become the most important weapon among Indians trading with the English and Dutch, then musket use by these tribes would surely have been universal by the time of their war with the English in 1675–76. We will look at the evidence for the use of muskets by all Native combatants in King Philip's War, including the Mohawk, Narragansett, Wampanoag, and Nipmuck. We will attempt to establish whether compelling evidence exists for the theory that there were large numbers of guns in Indian hands, and also whether there is evidence for the development of trade-dependence based upon the personal firearm during this period.

By the third quarter of the century, the possibility that aboriginals might acquire enough guns along with expertise in their use and maintenance to overrun the colonists was beginning to be perceived as a real threat. In 1662, when Major Winslow seized the Wampanoag Chief Alexander and his eight companions, the latter had "newly come in from hunting, and had left their Guns without Doors." (Hubbard 1974, Mather 1972:70) During the 1660s we see frequent reference to guns in the possession of New England Natives. The colonists' anxiety about them, of which

Alexander's seizure was a symptom, continued. The English also continued to handle the situation badly. In 1671 the new chief of the Wampanoag, Metacomet ("King Philip," brother of "Alexander"), visited Plymouth with a retinue of warriors. Philip disclaimed all hostile designs and promised future alliance (Knowles 1934). He was treated rather condescendingly and was forced to surrender his party's armament of "about seventy guns, as proof of his sincerity." (Thomson 1887:38) It is likely that these seventy guns represented a high percentage of Metacomet's stock of firearms, probably assembled to present a show of force to the British. Apparently their loss took about four years to make good (Thomson 1887:38, Knowles 1934). If firearms were plentiful enough to supply the thousands of warriors whom Metacomet eventually led (Hubbard 1974:55, Knowles 1934:341), then we would assume that the loss of seventy or so would hardly delay a war for four years, as Knowles suggests. In fact, it seems more likely that the four-year delay had little to do with a lack of guns. The significant loss at Plymouth may have been prestige rather than technology. We do know, from the Plymouth records, where Philip acquired the guns he surrendered; the agreement he signed read: "to remove all suspicion we voluntarily agree to deliver up to them *all the fire-arms* which they have heretofore kindly presented us with, until such time as they can safely repose confidence in us." [Signed by Philip and four Chief men in presence of the Governor and Council, 1671] (Trumbull 1846:63–66, italics mine)

We might also ask why Philip so readily surrendered these weapons if he considered them vital for warfare. We have no adequate account of these 1671 events, but might speculate that either Philip was well enough armed that he could afford to lose the weapons, or that he had brought them to impress the English, but did not feel that their loss was so great a burden that he would risk a confrontation to prevent it. The suggestion in this latter case is that the gun might have been perceived by the Natives as efficacious less for its utility as a weapon than for its psychological impact on the minds of Europeans, whose experience with this technology derived from the more useful context of the European battlefield. This argument will be further elaborated in the final chapter of this work. I have suggested earlier that the proliferation of guns among the Natives did not really get under way until after 1650. It would appear from the foregoing evidence that this process of armament was by no means complete by 1675, but continued well into the eighteenth century.

The task of estimating the significance of the firearm in Native warfare after 1650 is made difficult by the lack of attention paid by our informants to these kinds of details. The fact that these writers were usually describing events which had happened somewhat earlier (for example, Mather 1972, Hubbard 1974, Church 1772) and in which they were not direct participants, increases the danger that these details, where present, are abstracted from the author's experience rather than the accounts of his informants. Nevertheless, we have little choice but to proceed, making maximum use of available archival material.

Most of the New England material which refers to earlier periods (for example, the Pequot war of 1637 and Iroquois War period) was written closer to the time of King Philip's War (for example, Mather 1972, Saltonstall 1966, Church 1772, Drake 1975). We might expect that the accuracy of these writers with regard to the temporal specificity of weapons types will be best for this later period. We might also expect that inaccuracy due to cross-temporal generalization would be much more likely for the earlier periods. Thus it is conceivable that a given author might present a description of several temporally disparate events in such a way that in many details these separate episodes appear to be quite similar. This sort of projection will, of course, be most likely where the author "fills in" details of their narrative which may have been borrowed from the period of the writing. This borrowing is especially likely where the author does not perceive the period of the events described as distinctly different from his own period. Lacking objective data it is understandable that the author might generalize details of situations from the present to "adjacent" periods where structurally similar situations existed. Thus it is that the descriptions offered by Church, Mather and Saltonstall reveal relatively little change between the period 1640–1650 and 1675.

A second, less subtle bias is evident in this narrative material. The New Englanders who bemoaned the extensive gun trade of the Dutch and French from whom they were geographically far removed, saw heretic Antinomians, demonic Quakers and over two hundred witches at their own doorstep (Erikson 1966). The same English Puritans saw the Jesuits as the embodiment of "vile popery" (Mather 1972, Rowlandson 1962) and naturally believed that they were arming the Natives who, of course, worshipped the devil. The French Jesuits blamed the Protestants, not entirely unfairly, for arming the Mohawk (Mather 1972, Trigger 1976:628). Doubtless all colonies engaged in the gun trade, and all blamed the others somewhat unfairly. As was suggested earlier, the colonists' estimates of the illicit trade for which they were responsible are not to be accepted uncritically. How much less credence should we give their statements about the forbidden trade practised by the other colonies?

We will first explore the archival data which may be interpreted as indicating that the firearm had become the dominant weapon among New England Natives by 1675. We will then examine the case against that proposition.

Some of the most convincing evidence of Native gun use is that which pertains to the existence of Native maintenance or repair facilities. It is unlikely that weapons would remain operational for long if they could not be repaired, and equally unlikely that repair forges would exist where relatively few guns were in use.

Bradford tells us that not only did the Natives have all sorts of bullet molds (as would any settler who had a gun) but that some could mend and new-stock a gun as early as 1655 (Burke 1967:30). His statement is borne out by the case, mentioned earlier, where Joseph Jones of Massachusetts traded a Native a musket with a broken stock and a defective barrel for a new barrel (Mass. Archives 30:63–64). It is apparent that this Native sought a functioning lock, which along with a barrel and stock, could be used to make a gun. Mayer (1943) makes much of this incident, suggesting that it indicates considerable familiarity and skill on the part of the Natives. In the opinion of this author such conclusions are quite unwarranted. These weapons are very simple in construction.[1] Even the new-stocking of a musket would require little thought, and no new techniques for people who were in the habit of making their own tools and weapons of wood and stone. We must remember in this regard that the ordinary snaphaunces and flintlocks of the seventeenth century were crudely executed. The stocks are roughly hewn, sharp edged, and square in appearance, a far cry from the graceful flowing lines and compound curves of the flintlocks of the 1700s such as the British "Brown Bess" or French "Charleville."

By the 1670s however, we have genuine indications that Natives had developed a gun repair technology. During the 1660s the New England colonists, as part of the effort to "civilize" the Natives, had encouraged many to apprentice themselves to tradesmen (Malone 1973:54–5). While it was forbidden, still, to teach Natives how to make or repair guns (Malone 1973:57), it is not unreasonable to assume that, for a member of such a small community, exposure to the tools and techniques of the gunsmith (who was often also the blacksmith as well) would be frequent. I would suggest that those Native gunsmiths whom we hear about in the 1670s received their training during the 1660s when they were encouraged to become members of English communities.

---

[1] It took me less than twenty minutes to discover how to disassemble and reassemble a true flintlock. It is entirely reasonable to assume that a person who had any experience with firearms would be able to put one together from parts. It is to be noted, in fairness to Mayer, that gun components were individually fitted and were not interchangeable without modification.

We know that some Natives did become capable blacksmiths and specialized in weapons, including guns (Malone 1973:57, Saltonstall 1966–6:59, Mayer 1943:33–34, Hamilton 1968:103–07, Bradford 1952:82). In 1670, Hugh Coles of Swansea visited the Wampanoag at Mt. Hope and noted the presence of Narragansett craftsmen who were repairing Wampanoag firearms as well as making other types of weapons (Coles 1973:1, Saltonstall 1966–6:59, Leach 1958:26). This bears out testimony that the Narragansett in 1670 had at least one forge, at Rhode Island (Malone 1973:58). It seems, however, that the Narragansett may have had few such blacksmiths. When the English destroyed their major stronghold in the Great Swamp Battle of 1675, they killed a "Native black-smith (the only man amongst them that fitted their guns and arrow-heads)." (Saltonstall 1966–6:59) This individual was not, however, the only smith. When Captain Turner led his Massachusetts soldiers against a camp on the Connecticut River in May of the next year, they "demolished two forges they had to mend their arms; took away all their materials and tools . . . and threw two great pigs of lead of theirs (intended for making of bullets) into the said river." (Saltonstall 1966–6:96)

Another type of evidence for the widespread incorporation of the firearm into Native material culture is its acquiring a symbolic function in ritual. I found two examples of the gun as war-related symbol. Mary Rowlandson, in her narrative of captivity among the Wampanoag, describes the use of guns as weapons-symbols in a pow-wow in preparation for their attack at Sudbury (Rowlandson 1962:76). As early as 1666 we hear of the use of the gun as symbol: "if there be only wounded, they paint a broken gun which, however is connected with the stock, or even an arrow." (O'Callaghan 1849:6)

As early as 1662 when Chief Alexander of the Wampanoag was seized so ungraciously by Major Winslow, he and his eight companions may have constituted an elite group, likely to have guns as early as they were available. By 1667 the Wampanoag had enough guns that the General Court at Plymouth felt obliged to seize them when trouble was expected (Leach 1958:25). We know also that Philip was able to surrender 70 guns in 1671 and that the English demanded that "the rest" of his guns also be surrendered. The remaining guns, how many we do not know, were not turned in. If it took several years to replace the 70 (Thomson 1887:38), the number must have been small. As suggested earlier, Philip may have brought most of his arsenal to Plymouth as a display of force.

The Wampanoag used some guns in their attack on Lancaster on February 10, 1675. During the same month, a "praying Native" traded a gun for Mary Rowlandson's child and there was some talk of trading Rowlandson for powder at Albany. Rowlandson also tells us that Philip's men were on their way to get powder from the French when they were attacked by the Mohawk and obviously thought of the gun as the common Wampanoag weapon. In July of 1675 we hear that a White emissary to the Nipmuck country met a party of warriors who "cocked their guns at him" and that "guns were aimed at him." (Ellis and Morris 1906:84–86) This same emissary was informed by the Quabaugs' Chief Mutaump and by Chief Uskatukgun (Sagamore Sam) of the Nashaway that they would believe neither he nor his masters until they received 3 bushels of powder (Rowlandson 1962:42–44,49,59,66,78,87).

We find several accounts wherein Europeans attributed Native victory to the gun. On January 6, 1675, Capt. Holyoke's son and 20 men attacked a group of Natives outside Springfield: "The Natives, being furnished with muskets, were unwilling to give ground, and would probably have remained masters of the field of battle." (Trumbull 1846:78) In 1676 the fugitive Wampanoag were attacked by the Mohawk on March 5 in the latter's territory. "The engagement was a serious one. The fugitive Natives being provided with firearms, repelled the attack." (Trumbull 1846:85)

During an attack on Lancaster in July of 1676, Major Savage dispatched three companies of cavalry to the rescue. The soldiers contrived to get lost and ended up in the midst of 350 Natives who surrounded them. The English fought for some time, but: "the savages, being, however, well-provided with fire-arms, soon gained a complete victory." Before this attack, friendly Natives returning to Boston had warned the English that a large body of the enemy were seen: "in a wood near Lancaster, which village they intended to attack and burn in a few days: that they had been encouraged to continue the war with the English by Frenchmen from the great lake, who had supplied them with fire-arms and ammunition." (Trumbull 1846:78)

There are a number of accounts which refer to large numbers of guns in the hands of Natives. In 1675, Captain Church and his band attempted to assault Philip's stronghold at Mt. Hope. Apparently the intrepid New Englanders hoped he was off marauding somewhere, for when a group of Church's men discovered that the Natives were prepared to resist, they retreated across the river. A rather comical scene followed wherein Church remained on the Native side of the river and tried to convince these men to join him:

> And while he stood calling and persuading, the skulking enemy returned to their old stand; and all discharged their guns at him at one clap; and though every shot missed him, yet one of the army on the other side of the river received one of the balls in his foot. (Church 1772:33)

Later in 1675, Church was marching with his men when they were at-tacked:

> But before they saw anybody they were saluted with a volley of fifty or sixty guns. Some bullets came very surpris-ingly near Mr. Church, who, starting, looked behind him to see what was become of his men . . . but seeing them all upon their legs and briskly firing at the smokes of the enemy's guns (for that was all that was then to be seen) . . . (Church 1772:41–42)

Church reports "casting his eyes to the hill above them, the hill seemed to move, being covered with Natives with their bright guns glittering in the sun" who "hailed them with a shower of bullets." (Church 1772:42–43) I must point out here that the gun barrels of this period were not blued, or otherwise coated to prevent rust. Guns of the day were either chemically rusted, or allowed to rust naturally. In any case it is unlikely that any gun would "glitter in the sun" unless it was very new.

In 1676, Philip, himself carrying a gun, was shot with two balls by a Mohegan. His captain, Annawon, surrendered his arms to Church "both their guns and hatchets etc." (Church 1772:123,139) On the basis of these reports it would appear that the gun was the primary weapon in Native warfare. This is the sort of stuff of which dependency theories are made. Before we conclude that Natives had converted entirely to the firearm by 1675, let us look at the obverse side of the coin. We will focus on the same geographical area, and the same set of battles, looking at data which may be counter-indicative of firearms predominance.

Evidence Against the Native Use of Firearms

Philip was able to field about four thousand warriors (Hubbard 1974:55, Thomson 1887:39), although probably half of these were other Natives within his influence (Knowles 1934:341). Thousands of other warriors from the Narragansett and their allies also joined the fray after the war was under way. Significant armament would, therefore, consist in thousands of guns. Little evidence can be found of such numbers.

We find numerous accounts of battles where few, if any, firearms were used by the Natives. In 1672, Captain Church and his men were ambushed, receiving first a volley of arrows, and then a knife and toma-hawk charge (Trumbull 1846:67). This is the pattern of most Native attacks, whether bow or gun was used, as I have argued in an earlier section. Europeans also engaged in this sort of attack. At Brookfield, for example, Major Willard pressed home his numerical advantage and "rushed upon the savages with clubbed muskets." (Trumbull 1846:67, 69) The musket, despite its limitations as a projectile weapon, was very useful as a club. The Sachem Pompham, was killed in this way on September 16, 1676 (Trumbull 1846:90).

As mentioned earlier, Church was attacked with arrows, tomahawks and knives in 1672, prior to King Philip's War. Nor did Native use of guns increase by the time of the war. On March 6, 1675, Captains Pierce and Watkins attacked a small group of Natives near Patuxet. This group turned out to be a decoy and the English were surrounded by five hundred Natives: "They with their tomahawks and scalping knives rushed furiously upon them, threatening them with instant destruction." (Trumbull 1846:72)

During the year 1675–76, volunteer English companies formed in Connecticut, in New London, Norwich and Stonington. These groups were associated with several Native allies. Between spring and fall 1675, they made ten or more expeditions during which they killed or captured 230 of the enemy and stole 160 bushels of their corn. Although they overcame so many of the enemy and drove the numerous Narragansett tribes (save that of Ninnegret) from their homeland, the English managed to capture only 50 muskets (Thomson 1887:43).

Let us examine the evidence from the largest battle of the war. This took place at Philip's headquarters and Metacomet himself barely escaped. On December 7, 1676, the combined forces of the United Colonies attacked Philip's winter encampment. They were accompanied in the attack by Mohegan allies, including Oneco, son of the Sachem Uncas (Trumbull 1846:72). After an initial skirmish, the Wampanoag and Narragansett allies retreated into a strong and well designed fort, built by Stonewall John, a Narragansett who had studied masonry with the English (Malone 1973:60). With sixty picked men, Oneco ascended to the top of the fort, where he and his men . . . having a fair chance of the enemy . . . hurled their tomahawks and discharged their arrows with such success among them, as in a very short time to throw them into the utmost confusion." Of 4,000 Wampanoags, only 200, including Metacomet, escaped. The British, ignoring pleas for quarter, mounted the walls and fired volley upon volley into the trapped Natives. The British lost at least five officers, including Captains Davenport, Seely and Gardner, and 299 men, as well as 513 wounded. Twelve companies had entered the battle on the English side (Trumbull 1846:72). There is no indication that the Natives on either side, even the close allies of the English, made significant use of the gun.

At the battle of Hatfield, February 10, 1676, the Natives lay flat on the ground: "as they were accustomed to do on the approach of the English . . . until the latter had advanced within bowshot, when, partly rising, they discharged a shower of *arrows* among them, which wounded several of the

English." (Trumbull 1846:85 italics mine) Similarly, on September 16, 1676, hatchets were the only weapons among the Sachem Pompham's 100 men, women and children who were massacred by the numerically superior British headed by Captains Mosely and Brattle as well as Major Bradford at Dedham. At the battle near Pomfret on October 12, 1676, the Natives fired arrows from concealment, and then attacked the English with knives and tomahawks (Trumbull 1846:90). Neither side used guns on November 2 of the same year, when Boston's troops fought the Kennebeck and Amsocoggin at Newchewannick, near the Kennebeck River, employing cutlasses against tomahawks (Trumbull 1846:93,96).

Near this site, Majors Wallace and Bradford and 6 companies of men attacked the main body of about 800 of the enemy on December 3. The Natives "were in possession of but few firearms, but hurled their tomahawks with inconceivable exactness, and checked the progress of the cavalry with long spears." Despite their lack of firearms, the Natives would probably have won this battle had English reinforcements not arrived (Trumbull 1846:96). On March 22, 1676, a "Negro" who had been imprisoned by Metacomet's men escaped and warned the English of an impending attack. Apparently Philip planned to attack Taunton and adjacent villages. For this purpose he had assembled a body of 1,000 warriors, and "near one hundred of them were furnished with fire-arms." (Trumbull 1846:86)

In view of the preceding evidence, the above figure of less than 10 percent of Native warriors in possession of guns by 1676 may not be unreasonable. This proportion would still allow that many hundreds of guns had been sold legally or illegally in the preceding few years. We will now examine some aspects of musket use which may help us to understand: firstly, why some Natives may have never used, or ceased to use firearms; and secondly, how we may reconcile the volume of the gun trade implied by Trigger (1976), Tooker (1963), and Otterbein (1965) with the evidence suggesting that gun use was far from universal.

Lacking ideal cleaning facilities, guns which burn black powder will last a very short time; black powder is a highly corrosive compound. The only way to keep such a weapon operational is to flush it repeatedly with hot water and soap as soon after firing as possible. If allowed to sit for even one night, the fouling inside the barrel will have combined with moisture in the air to form a sludge reminiscent of the inside of a dirty oven. If not completely removed (a thoroughly unpleasant task), the residue will corrode the bore very quickly. Even more importantly, as I found to my chagrin during the experimental phase of this project, it is virtually impossible to fire the weapon until it is cleaned. The dry, caked fouling, which had merely prevented one from loading the ball the day before, was now a thick black sludge which moistens powder, plugs up touch-hole, lubricates flint and frizzen so they refuse to spark, and prevents the seating of the ball. To properly clean a musket takes about twenty minutes if one is equipped with a cleaning kit (scourer, cloth patches, threaded ramrod) as well as concentrated detergent, hot running water and oil to coat the bore after it is dry. The tenacity with which black powder fouling adheres to and rusts any metal surface is better experienced than discussed.

Even during the shooting session, especially if the weather is humid, it is necessary to clear the touch-hole and wipe off the flint and frizzen every shot or two, and to "ream" the bore with a bore brush, at first after four to six discharges, and then after every two to four shots (this varies with the size of ball used). If the gun is not wiped off, it will misfire frequently, and if the bore is not cleaned, its reduced internal diameter will prevent the ball from seating on the powder. Having firmly lodged the ball half-way down the barrel in attempts to seat it, the shooter has little choice but to find a "bullet screw" and extract it.

My experience with these weapons while researching for the present work has convinced me that King Philip's warriors would have found them to be close to useless for the type of warfare in which they engaged by 1676. If they had been operating from an established base, with access to well-equipped gunsmiths, the problems of firearms maintenance would be manageable. However, by 1676 the army of Philip was reduced to roving bands, unable to establish stable villages. Such an army would have had difficulty keeping the weapons operational. To these problems must be added the difficulties encountered in obtaining powder and lead. Unlike the Natives, Europeans had few bows and little choice but to use the gun.

How can we explain that relatively few, say 10 percent, of the Natives participating in the war of 1675–76 were armed with guns after over 20-years of brisk gun trade? It should be noted that few authors have attempted to estimate the actual volume of trade. Hunt (1972), Trigger (1976) and Tooker (1963) use the number 400 guns in the hands of the Mohawk in 1644 and argue that this was only the beginning. The trade, while of scandalous proportions as early as 1649, was not necessarily voluminous relative to the thousands of potential consumers. Where, as in New Amsterdam, such trade was banned under pain of death (Mayer 1943:49), ten individuals smuggling a few guns each to the Natives would be quite disturbing, doubly so as local Natives would be the most likely customers. For example, when, in an attempt to become the main supplier of guns, the Council of New Netherland imported 100 guns (Resolution of the States General, April 11, 1650), some or all of which were traded to Natives, the colonists were most alarmed, and noticed a definite increase in the number of guns possessed by Natives: "Whilst your Honours' disrespect caused both the stamped and other guns to be sold to the Natives, who were seen running all over the Manhattans with some of them." (Letter from Lubert von Duecklage, 1651, in Mayer 1943:53) Thus it is possible that the trading of relatively few guns could have sufficiently scandalized the colonists that they, being sensitive to the prospect of their own demise, might have complained.

Some authors have suggested that Native people took no care of their guns, so that they soon wore out from sheer abuse (Russell 1957, Gooding 1962). There is, however, substantial evidence that Natives were quick to acquire many of the necessary skills to maintain their weapons (Bradford in Burke 1967:30). It is not necessary to denigrate Native culture in order to suggest that guns did not last long in their hands.

Firstly, flint guns, especially snaphaunces, are easy to damage; even in normal use, parts such as sears, mainsprings, feather-springs, cocks or frizzens either wear out or break. If replacement parts are unavailable, the weapon becomes useless. We have little useful data regarding the trade in spare parts though we do know that such trade was also forbidden. We know that as early as 1655 the Narragansett could thread a screw or new-stock a gun (Bradford in Burke 1967:30), and we know that they had a forge by 1675 (Saltonstall 1966–6:59). The Iroquois do not appear to have developed the skills to repair muskets. Puype states that "a very small number of gunsmithing implements as well as an absolute lack of forging tools suggests that there were few if any specialized gun-makers among the Indians" and argues that this hypothesis is supported by historical evidence (Puype 1985:91). We can be quite certain that Native craftsmen could not manufacture a mainspring or a frizzen. The evidence suggests that Native gun repair consisted of recombining parts of broken guns to make functioning ones, with resulting attrition.

Secondly, without very thorough and regular cleaning, it is unlikely that a black powder gun would last longer than three years (Chown 1976–77). From my experience, I would be surprised if a musket used outside and stored in Native villages and hunting camps would survive for that long.

If we suppose that the average gun was in service for three years, and further that even 10 percent of all warriors of the Iroquois, Huron, Ottawa, Wampanoag, Narragansett and Mohegan tribes had firearms, we can speculate about the volume of trade required to maintain this level of armament. These tribes and their close allies could surely field more than 10,000 warriors (the accuracy of this figure is of minimal importance — I use it hypothetically). Given this number of warriors, 1,000 guns would be required to arm 10 percent. To maintain this level of armament, more than 300 guns would have to be acquired each year. If 1 in 5 warriors wished to maintain a gun between 1665 and 1675, 6,600 weapons would have to be acquired, or an average of 660 per year. In suggesting that every warrior had a gun by 1665 we are assuming, given our starting figures, that 33,000 guns were acquired (or rebuilt) during the decade before 1675.

I wish to make clear that I present this *reductio ad absurdum* argument to illustrate the fact that, even if we knew how many guns were sold each year by each colony, we could not simply add up the numbers. We have no adequate data on which to base precise estimates. Illegal gun-traders left few records, and those colonists who did saw an Native behind every tree and a gun in the hands of every Native. It would seem, however, that even by 1675 the firearm was a minor factor in Native warfare, so minor in fact as to render dependency hypotheses untenable for this period. Serious implementation of firearms use in warfare or dependency on firearms by any Natives prior to the Iroquois wars (1648–52) is, therefore, most unlikely.

Even by 1675 there is little evidence to support the contention that any Native group had acquired enough guns to consider themselves militarily dependent on them. At this late date, projectile weapons still played a significant but not a dominant role in Indian warfare. Most battles were won through hand to hand combat. The weapons trade only began in earnest during the fifth decade of the seventeenth century. It seems very unlikely that after, at most, eight years of this trade (that is, by 1648) any Native group was well provided with flintlocks, when this was certainly not the case even twenty-seven years later.

Chapter Seven

The Musket – Operational Parameters

The purpose of this chapter is to establish as clearly as possible the operational parameters of seventeenth century muskets which might have reached Native people. The musket's use was not, of course, restricted to the casting of projectiles; it was also used as club, spear or noisemaker. It may also have functioned as a powerful symbol. However I am concerned here with the performance of European versus aboriginal projectile weapons in terms of their most obvious and concrete function.

Several factors are focused on experimentally in this chapter, including accurate and also lethal range, rate of fire, and short-term reliability (i.e., misfire rate). Other factors were not examined experimentally, but are discussed with reference to the literature. These include long-term reliability (ie., frequency of repair), useful life, ease of repair, operational requirements (ie., need for powder, arrows, etc.), ease of acquisition, and ease of handling (for example, portability, convenience and compatibility with other weapons).

To provide a basis for comparison, I will discuss the capabilities of the Native bow with reference to the literature. The point here is to determine whether the gun offered distinct advantages over the bow as a projectile weapon. Even if it did not, this says nothing conclusive about Native-perceived efficacy, or dependency. Nevertheless I suggest that the onus shifts to proponents of the dependency hypothesis to show how such non-rational dependency developed and was maintained.

The "experimental archaeology" (Coles 1973) part of the research involved testing a total of six muskets over a period of one year. Several kinds of tests were conducted at a rifle range in the Ottawa area. I used the weapons with various sorts of projectiles, at ranges from 15 to 200 yards, during all seasons and all types of weather. The testing was aimed primarily at determining the capabilities and limitations of the weapons themselves, independent of the skill of the user. Some data, such as range and accuracy were derived experimentally in the formal sense of the word and will be presented as such. Other data, such as ease of handling and accuracy, where marksmanship is not controlled for, are necessarily anecdotal.

With any firearm, it is necessary to develop a "load" which produces best performance. For every individual gun a slightly different combination of powder charge, wadding, and projectile will be required to obtain maximum accuracy (Nonte 1976, Ramage 1975, Kirkland 1972). Where factors other than accuracy, such as range or force of impact (or, in the case of a muzzle-loader, speed of loading) are important, this load will represent a compromise among these factors and accuracy. This is true also for modern cartridge weapons (hence the widespread practice of "handloading" cartridges among target shooters). The weapons used for this testing were "shot-in" in this sense. I cannot claim to have developed an optimal load for each gun, but feel that these test results are as good or better than those obtained by users in the seventeenth century.

It is necessary to discuss some of the differences between my weapons and supplies and those available in North America in the seventeenth century.

The Gunpowder

The process of the manufacture of "black powder" propellant evolved continuously throughout its centuries of use, parallel to the development of the guns in which it was used. The gunpowder of Berthold and Bacon was a simple mixture of common charcoal, saltpetre and sulphur. Most experiments prior to 1700 involved changes in the proportions of the various ingredients to produce either more power or greater stability (at the expense of power). One of the most annoying properties of early gunpowder, referred to as "serpentine powder," was its tendency to separate into three layers according to the specific gravities of the ingredients (Cotterman 1972, Held 1970). Another disadvantage was its sensitivity to bullet seating pressure. If the ball compressed the fine powder too much, ignition was only partial. If the ball was not seated in contact with the powder, there was danger of blowing up the piece. Anyone who has loaded a musket, especially one with a fouled (and therefore tight) barrel, can attest to the difficulty of seating the ball on the powder such that contact is assured, but also seating it so delicately as to compress the powder only a little.

Some of the disadvantages of serpentine powder were eliminated by the process of "corning," whereby the mixture was wetted and baked into a solid cake, and then sifted to granulate it. This is a gross simplification of what became a highly complex process, the description of which would take several pages (see Une 1846:620–29).

Being a compound, corned powder does not separate into its constituents, nor is it as sensitive to compression as serpentine powder. Additionally, varying the grain size controls the rate at which the powder burns. The faster burning coarse powders are used in weapons with a lower bore-size to barrel-length ratio and finer powders are used where barrels are longer relative to bore size. By using a powder of the correct granulation, the gunman assures that all of the powder burns while the bullet is still travelling down the barrel, and its energy is converted into the increased velocity of the projectile. The longer the barrel, the slower burning the powder needed to be to continuously accelerate the bullet down its length. A shorter barrel requires a granulation fast-burning enough that all of the powder's energy may act upon the projectile before it leaves the barrel.

Although the manufacture of corned powder was understood as early as 1600, its use only became universal in Europe after 1700 (Leblonde 1970). In his treatise of 1743, Leblonde tells us that corned powder was not used for guns before the eighteenth century because it was too powerful (it created excessive barrel pressures). Leblonde's book deals with heavy ordinance, and it might be argued that his remarks may have applied less to small-arms. Since some of the weapons he discusses have bore sizes of only one inch, which is the size of a shoulder-fired wall-gun and only 25 percent larger than many standard military hand-held weapons, his remarks concerning powder probably applied equally to muskets.

It seems likely then that modern, corned gunpowder which I used in these tests was much superior to that available in the 1600s. Even if Native North Americans did not use serpentine powder, we can be very sure that at best their powder was manufactured using one of the less complex and less adequate processes which evolved prior to 1700. We also know that the Natives' gunpowder was all brought from Europe, the first North American powder mill being established by the British in 1675. Remembering the affinity of black powder for moisture, we may speculate that the long sea voyage and storage problems in the New World caused much of this powder to spoil.

The powder used in this testing was purchased from the only two manufacturers of black powder in North America. Not only is it properly corned and labelled as to grain sizes (for example, Fg being the coarsest, FFg and FFFg being medium gradations and FFFFg being the finest), but each grain is coated with graphite to increase resistance to moisture. Needless to say, in a day when many European gunners were still expected to make their own powder, these niceties were non-existent. Thus, the powder used in these tests was much more powerful (therefore produced greater range), consistent (resulting in greater accuracy), drier, and more moisture resistant (resulting in greater reliability) than any powder a European or Native gunner could have hoped to obtain. The range, accuracy, and reliability of ignition it produced must be considered a theoretical ideal from the point of view of a seventeenth-century European gunner, let alone the Native trader.

I originally planned to manufacture and test powder made according to an early process. After considerable research, I decided to forego this part of the experiment because no formula and process could accurately be dated as typical for the period in question. The expense and peril involved in the milling of powder (Held 1970) dissuaded me from attempting to produce any formula until its use by Native people in the seventeenth century could be demonstrated.

The Projectile

The projectiles used during this experiment were all cast by the author. I used a "precision melter" designed to heat lead for the casting of bullets. Procedures for bullet casting appearing in several modern texts on the subject (for example, Nonte 1976:98, Ramage 1975:55–59) were rigidly adhered to. For the most part, the bullet molds were modern block-type, much more precise than early scissors-type molds. Two such early molds were also used, however.

There are several variables which may affect the accuracy of a musket ball. First is its size relative to that of the barrel which directs its path. If the ball is loose, it ricochets down the barrel and its angle of exit will vary. However, a ball which is too large, while it may provide one or two accurate shots, will lodge firmly in the barrel once the latter begins to foul. We know that all military gunners used balls with approximately 1/24 to 1/16 in. "windage" (the difference in size between ball and bore). It is plausible, however, that since European hunters were aware of the advantages of a tight-fitting ball, some larger molds may have reached this continent. Again, accurate data is non-existent: we have a few bullet molds found by archaeologists, but have no idea what size of bore their balls were fired from. I chose to err on the positive side, using tighter fitting projectiles where a choice was possible. To allow comparison, I also used loose as well as tight fitting projectiles in the 0.75 cal musket.

During the 1600s it was common practice to leave the "sprue" (the stubble of lead attached to the ball, molded by the opening through which the lead was poured into the spherical cavity of the bullet mold) attached to the ball. While this appendage greatly unbalanced the ball, dramatically reducing accuracy (with a smooth-bore weapon the projectile does not gyro-stabilize), it was handy because one could tie a paper "cartouche" containing powder to it with string. Little was known of ballistics, and shooters probably felt that any trade-off was advantageous. While a sprue cutter was used to trim most of the balls used in the following tests, the reader might bear in mind that according to a brief initial test, shooting balls with sprue attached increased the "group size" by about 50 percent. From Champlain's battle of 1609 to the death of Metacomet in 1676, multiple shot was also used for warfare in North America. I see little evidence to suggest widespread military use of multiple projectiles, but elected to conduct tests of its efficacy as well.

Other Factors

The flints used in testing were purchased from five different suppliers. They varied somewhat in size, shape, colour and quality of napping. This may be the one area where my equipment was inferior to that of the seventeenth century. Perhaps when the art of flint napping was more widespread, better quality flints were available. As the quality of the flint does affect the likelihood that the primer will ignite, it is wise to bear these considerations in mind.

In order to provide a pressure seal, and also to fit the ball tightly to the barrel, some sort of "patching" has been used in muskets since their development. The best practice (to obtain maximum accuracy and range) is to wrap the ball in cloth such that the size of ball with its wrapping is just slightly larger than the bore. The patch, prior to its fitting, must be lubricated with grease, or, if the shot is to be fired immediately, with saliva. The optimal patching material is pure Irish linen, which does not readily burn and so accompanies the bullet until it leaves the barrel. To use such a patch, it is first lubricated and then placed over the muzzle of the gun, the ball is set on top, and ball with cloth are "thumbed" into the muzzle until the top of the ball is slightly above it; the patch is then trimmed, so that no excess remains. The ball with its (now) circular patch is ready to be rammed home. In keeping with my policy to err on the positive side where precise data regarding Native practices is unavailable, I used this technique with Irish linen patching, with both modern patch grease and my own saliva as lubricant. Such finesse was seldom evident among the seventeenth-century Europeans who were more likely to cram a loose fitting ball down the bore, accompanied by paper, cloth, or whatever else would help it stay there. To facilitate comparison of techniques, again using the 0.75 cal musket, I shot not only 0.730 and 0.735 in. balls with linen patching, but also used the standard British military loading system employed in the early 1700s. This latter system employed a coarse paper tube containing both ball and powder (the British used a 100-gr charge). The end of the tube was bitten off, and about 20 gr used to prime while the remainder of the powder was poured down the barrel. The paper, with ball enclosed, was then rammed home (Held 1970). At best, the paper provided a short-lived gas seal, and did little to "fit" the ball to the bore. The lack of seal was particularly unfortunate because the British (and I) used a ball only 0.690 in. in diameter. That is over 1/16 in. windage!

Where many shooters, (for example, the British military) merely used a little of their main charge powder for priming, I used a finer powder for better ignition, a practice which was also common (Held 1970, Kirkland 1972). Further, I precisely measured all powder charges so that consistency and therefore accuracy would be maximized.

Where, under battle conditions, it might be necessary to fire many times without cleaning, I allowed myself the luxury of cleaning the bore with a wire brush after every three shots (save during barrel fouling tests). This was done partly to ensure maximum accuracy and partly to spare myself the embarrassment of having a ball jam three quarters of the way down the barrel. Despite this precaution, there were occasions when balls either had to be extracted with a bullet screw or the ramrod had to be tapped with a mallet to seat the ball on the powder.

Sighting and Holding Equipment

As late as 1850, many muskets were not fitted with sighting equipment of any kind. None had such equipment during the 1600s. Even the knob which appears at the muzzle of the Brown Bess (1703–1850) was meant to be a bayonet mounting stud. It could not be used as a sight with the bayonet attached as it would be in battle.

My interest was largely in determining what these weapons limits were, independent of user skill. For this reason, three of the guns were equipped with modern rear sights, using the knob at the front as a front sight. The 0.55 cal Spanish and 0.65 cal Enfield muskets were fitted with open style notch-type, non-adjustable sights (acceptable since "group size" rather than "point of aim" was our critical variable) while the 0.75 cal musket, as the main test weapon, was equipped with a small aperture fully adjustable receiver-type "William's peep sight." All of the guns were also fired with their original equipment, i.e., the knob at the muzzle.

Again, to eliminate as far as possible the shooter's skill as a variable, a shooting stand was employed. This device is a heavy tripod fitted such that it will cradle a rifle while allowing precise adjustment for aiming. When the sights are on target, the stand can be locked such that movement off-target is unlikely. The gun is fired in the usual manner at the shooter's shoulder. However, the shooter's main function is to absorb recoil and pull the trigger. Even the marked "flinch" many shooters develop when using flintlocks, especially those of such large bores, is unlikely to effect their accuracy. The weapons were also tested without the aid of the shooting stand.

Test Muskets

All of the guns fired during testing were modern replicas of antique weapons. A musket barrel is simply a straight metal tube, so the main difference between the test barrels and original weapons was strength. This was irrelevant for my purposes, as I had no intention of bursting them. It is, however, possible that the test barrels were a little more consistent in diameter due to modern manufacturing methods. The fragility and value of original weapons (for example, $6,000 or more for a plain military matchlock *circa* 1610) precluded their use for testing.

Because the range of bore sizes available in replica muskets is quite limited, it was necessary to use some guns with the more modern "percussion" ignition. It is unlikely that this ignition system would worsen the performance of the weapon; it should, however, greatly improve reliability. Where I discuss this variable, reference to the percussion gun's performance is mentioned separately, or is omitted.

The rest of the muskets are of the "true flintlock" type, the most modern and efficient of flint locks. For the testing of reliability, a snaphaunce or more primitive flintlock would have been preferable but could not be obtained. Accuracy and range were not affected, but we must regard the reliability of ignition with these locks as an ideal by seventeenth century standards.

I have identified the guns according to their country of origin (i.e. proof marks) and general style. The guns used were as follows:

Weapon	Bore	Bbl. Length	Lock-Type
Spanish fowling piece	0.55	28"	percussion
Belgian military type	0.56	41"	flint (later match)
Indian Enfield Musketoon	0.65	24"	percussion
Belgian trademusket	0.65	42"	flint
Belgian long-fowler	0.65	56"	flint
Italian Brown Bess	0.75	42"	flint

All of the weapons were smooth-bore. The 0.56 cal military-type musket (no. 2) was a flintlock, but due to shoddy workmanship, it had to be converted to matchlock in order to fire. The use of the match for which the lock was unsuited so frustrated my attempts at aiming that the weapon was retired. This incident illustrates my earlier argument that not even all true flintlocks were reliable weapons. (The distributor assures its customers that these weapons contain some "original" parts!)

By far the best made of these weapons, as well as the most representative of the period under study, is the 0.75 cal Brown Bess, a replica of the British Short Land Pattern "Common Musket" which, with minor variations, was the Arm of Empire from 1703 to 1850 (Held 1970, Darling 1970). This arm, made by Antonino Zoli of Italy, was much more reliable in terms of ignition than the other flintlocks. I also felt more confidence in its ability to contain the high pressures generated by heavier powder charges. This gun was equipped with the best sights and used as the main test weapon. The other guns were used mainly to determine whether or not bore size and barrel length were significant variables in a given test situation. The first test results to be discussed are those which represent the upper limit of musket performance.

Performance Tests

In order to measure the best accuracy and range obtainable with a smoothbore musket, I used the shooting stand (described earlier), tight fitting musket balls, linen patching, and modern sights. After initial experimentation to find the powder charges that gave best accuracy, over 100 test shots were fired from various distances.

Our interest is in "military accuracy," and for that reason I used a human-sized target. A 2.5-by-6.5-foot panel with a standard size archery target (to provide a central point of aim) was used for all testing. Range rules forbade the use of human silhouette targets or these would have been used. It should be remembered that few individuals approximate 2-by-6-foot dimensions and that few soldiers are so considerate as to present the full frontal target represented by the board we used; fewer still will remain in position long enough to allow such careful aim as was taken in these tests.

All of the muskets were capable of placing all shots within a 6-in. group at 25 yards. The best group was obtained with the 0.75 cal musket (no. 6) using a 0.735 ball with good cloth patches, an 80 gr charge of FFg powder, and FFFg primer. The group obtained was 4½ in. in diameter. It is possible that this accuracy could be improved somewhat, by using balls of identical weight, and by cleaning the bore after each shot. Sixty percent of the group was within 2½ in., while the other shots were distributed along the same vertical axis, but were above or below the central group, reflecting variance in projectile weights, inconsistency in loading, or other factors. It is clear from these results that at this short distance, the musket's accuracy was functionally equivalent to that of a more modern weapon (the practical difference between a 1/4-in. group and a 4 1/2-in. one has little import in military usage).

When the target was moved out to 50 yd, the groups began to spread out slightly. The best group was again obtained with the 0.75 cal musket (although by only a small margin). At this distance, using the 0.735 ball, cloth patch, a 90 gr charge of FFg powder and FFFg primer, a 13-in. group was consistently shot. Ten shot groups ranged from a best of 10 in. (no. 6 loaded as above) to a best of 18 in. with the .65 cal trade musket (no. 4) loaded with a 0.610 ball, tightly patched with Irish linen, propelled by 70 gr of FFg powder (this weapon had no rear sight however).

At 50 yd, under these ideal conditions, marginally acceptable military accuracy is retained, although with a spread of more than 1 ft, it is likely more "near misses" would occur where targets did not present a full frontal silhouette to the gunner. Even with a full frontal silhouette, shooter aiming-variance is more likely to place musket shots completely off-target than would be likely with a weapon capable of smaller groups.

At 75 yd about 80 percent of all shots grouped within 20 in. while 20 percent did not strike the 2-by-6-foot target area. It is difficult to determine the actual group size, as I was unable to place all of the balls from a single "string" of even 5 shots on the target board. The best group shot at this distance measured 18 in. However 2 of the 10 shots missed the board entirely. This group was shot with the .75 cal musket (no. 6), using 0.735 ball, and 90 gr powder charge, with cloth patch.

At 75 yd, while a military hit is likely, it is by no means a certainty. In these tests, fully 20 percent of all shots missed the 2-by-6-foot target board. Even under ideal conditions the effectiveness of a single musket against a more realistic target is doubtful at this distance.

At 100 yd the average group with muskets equipped with sights measured about 2 feet in diameter. A couple of 5 shot groups measuring about 18 in. were shot with the 0.75 cal musket (no. 6) loaded as before.

I am at a loss to explain why accuracy with the Brown Bess was better at 100 than at 75 yards. Tests at these ranges were conducted on different days. Perhaps I was somewhat more careful loading for the longer range, perhaps the musket balls were slightly more consistent in weight or shape (though selected at random). It may be the fact that these superior groups were shot at the beginning of the test day, with a completely clean gun, and that (having had an unnerving experience with a jammed ball) I cleaned the bore after each shot.

Next, a test was conducted using 2 of the weapons at a range of 200 yards. The report of results must be purely anecdotal because only about

1 in 10 shots hit the target board. No estimate of group size was possible, and I cannot be sure that my sights were adjusted such that the point of true aim was the centre of the target. With the aid of a helper who watched for signs that the balls were distributed evenly around the target, I estimated the group size to be over 10 ft and sighted-in the weapon as nearly as I could. It is obvious that unless used with mass volley tactics the musket is ineffective at this range.

In February 1860, the U.S. War Department, deliberating about which sort of gun to adopt as their new, standard military arm, compared smoothbore and rifled muskets using 10-by-10-foot targets at various distances (Fuller 1958). Trained American troops used these weapons, shooting in several ways (fire by volleys, by file, or as skirmishers). The tests are a good indication of what trained troops *circa* 1860 could do with the arms of their day. The War Department tested mostly rifled weapons, using the standard smoothbore as a basis for comparison. It is interesting that the War Department's results, with muskets, at the 200-yd range, though more comprehensive than my own, confirm my findings. Their best group was shot by ten soldiers, firing "as skirmishers." Of 50 shots, 24 struck the 10-by-10-foot target area, while only three hit within the 2-by-6-foot central area used in my tests. Six percent is not bad when we consider that I only achieved 10 percent with aid of the shooting stand and target sights! This means, however, that if ten trained soldiers fired at will at a 2-by-6-foot enemy at 200 yd, we would probably have to wait for a second volley for a hit. At 200 yd, firing "by volley," the results were even worse. Of 50 shots fired, only 18 struck the 10-by-10-foot board!

Having explored the musket's optimal performance, I conducted tests to estimate the level of accuracy obtainable with less than ideal projectiles and patching. Replicating the standard British load, similar to that used by all military gunmen during the seventeenth century, I prepared both coarse paper, and linen "cartouches." The musket used was a 0.75 cal British flintlock (no. 6) and the projectiles were 0.69 cal balls cast in two original scissors-type molds. The shooting stand, target sights, and careful loading procedures were used, as before. The powder charge was 90 gr FFg.

Where five 0.735 cal balls could be placed within 18 in. at 100 yd, the 0.690 projectiles performed somewhat worse. Only 60 percent (18 of 30) hit the 2-by-6-foot area. The group appeared to be about 4½ ft in diameter. Performances with cloth or paper cartridges or with bullets from either mold were equivocal. Accuracy was similarly reduced at closer ranges, although, of course, the weapon was more effective at close range.

At 100 yd, only 6 of 10 shots were likely to hit the 2-by-6-foot board, while at 75 yd, 80 percent struck the target board and these were all within the 2-by-3-foot centre. It is likely that all of the balls struck within a 3-by-3-foot area surrounding the point of aim. At 50 yd the projectiles formed a group measuring about 2 ft (accomplished with a 0.735 ball at 100 yd), while at 25 yd, most groups measured less than 10 in. (the best obtained with 0.735 ball at twice the distance). It would seem then, that using a standard military load, military accuracy is not obtainable at 50 yd, while at 100 yd only massed fire is likely to be effective. Tests were also conducted at 200 yd, but I was unable to place even a single shot on the target board at that distance.

The term "practical accuracy" refers to the likely performance of the weapons when shooting "offhand," that is to say, standing, with musket to shoulder, without the benefit of modern gunsights. The first test was conducted with the aid of the shooting stand, with the 0.65 cal trade musket (no. 4). Having "sighted-in" the gun-shooter combination (two shooters were trained to shoot with front sight only), a series of shots were fired which, in the judgement of the marksman, were aimed at the centre of the target.

I was surprised to find that at 25 yd, using an accurate patch/ball combination, one could train an inexperienced musketeer to shoot surprisingly well with only the front knob to guide them. With both 0.65 (no. 4) and 0.75 (no. 6) cal weapons, groups less than 1 ft in diameter were consistently obtained, provided that we were extremely careful to position the gun at our shoulders, and grip it in exactly the same manner every time. In this way, it was possible to place 40 percent of all shots on the 2-by-6-foot board at 100 yd though I must note that the use of the shooting stand eliminated inconsistency caused by movement while aiming or by the flinch which flintlock muskets engender in the user.

Next we shot the weapons (still without sights) from the "offhand" position without the aid of the stand. These, and the preceding data regarding performance without sights, are of course anecdotal, as the skill of the shooter was an important factor.

At 25 yd both I and a helper could "group" within 1½ ft fairly consistently. We usually hit the target board at 50 yd, usually missed it at 75, and were unable to hit it at all at 100 yards.

The 1860 American infantrymen apparently fared somewhat better, although it is likely that their guns were fitted with sights, and when firing "as skirmishers" they were allowed to assume more accurate positions than standing or "offhand." The War Department test results show that at 100 yd, using a smooth bore 0.69 cal musket (ball size is not reported), 10 soldiers could place 43 of 50 shots on a 10-ft-square target. Seventeen shots or 34 percent hit the 2-by-6-foot central section. I might add that these soldiers were using the percussion ignition system. The maximum accuracy of the gun is little affected by the lock type; however, that of the shooter most certainly is. The massive recoil of a large bore musket is enough, by itself, to bring about an anticipatory jerk or flinch as the trigger is pulled. Such a flinch may drastically reduce accuracy. One may, of course, gradually reduce or eliminate the flinch altogether through practice. Add to the recoil, however, the considerable delay between trigger pull, hammer-fall, flint sparking, primer ignition, main charge ignition, the smoke from the primer which obliterates the target, and the bits of burning gunpowder sprayed back into the face of the shooter, and the flinch is understandable. I doubt that many Native or European users without even the protection of shooting glasses (many particles were imbedded in mine) were able to "hold through" much better than we were.

In order to provide some semblance of experimental control, I shot several offhand groups with two, more accurate, weapons. The first was a muzzle-loading weapon of the large-bore, thin-barrelled type usually referred to as a "rifled musket" (as opposed to the thicker barrelled "muzzle loading rifle"). The gun in question is an excellent replica of the 0.58 cal Remington Contract Rifle (or "Zouave Rifle") used during the American Civil War. Using 0.575 round balls with linen patching, I was able to shoot 16-in. groups at one hundred yards from the standing position. With a borrowed, modern hunting rifle (.32 Winchester Mod. 94) 13-in. groups were average at the same distance. Typical results of my accuracy tests are summarized in the Table entitled Maximum Accuracy (see p. 105).

Various gun trials conducted during the nineteenth century tend to confirm my findings. Picard (Hughes 1974:3) reports that trained French soldiers, firing from a fixed rest at a 1.75 m. by 3.00 m. target could score 60 percent hits at 82 yards. Muller (Hughes 1974:64) tells us that using a target representing a line of cavalry, well trained soldiers could hit with 53 percent of their shots at 100 yd, 30 percent at 200 yd and 23 percent at 300 yards. Ordinary soldiers were able to score 40, 18 and 15 percent hits respectively. Using a 6-by-20-foot target (presumably representing massed enemy infantry) at 100 yd, 75 percent hits were reported by W.W. Greener (Hughes 1974:64) while 42 percent hit at 200 yd, 16 percent at 300 yd and 4.5 percent at 400 yards.

Because some mention appears in the archival record of the use of multiple shot (for example, Biggar 1896–1901:2:99, Mather 1972), this sort of load was also tested. Two to 6 pellets of "000 buckshot" (.375 cal balls) were loaded with cloth wadding over powder, and paper wadding to retain the shot in the barrel. At 25 yd, even where a 24 in. barrel was used, the shot spread only three inches on average, and lacked power, penetrating only 2 in. of dry pine. At this distance the chances of hitting the target were not improved, and the power of the weapon was considerably reduced. At 50 yd, 2 of 4, or 3 of 6 balls would hit the 2-by-6-foot target board although they were barely able to penetrate an inch of pine. These conclusions are supported by the fact that all military forces used solid balls. After moving the target to 100 yd I was unable to hit it placing 4 balls in my muskets.

Maximum Accuracy

(percent of hits on 2.5' by 6.5' target board)

Load Type	25 YD	50 YD	75 YD	100 YD	200 YD
Target load tight ball (.735 in 0.75 bore) shooting stand with rear sight fitted	100% (6" grp)	100% (13" grp)	80% (est. 18")	100% (est. 24")	10%
Military load loose ball (.69 in 0.75 bore) shooting stand	100% (10" grp)	100% (24" grp)	80% (est. 36" grp)	60% (est. 54" grp)	Negligible
Target load tight ball (12" grp) no rear sight shooting stand	100% (12" grp)	75%	55%	40%	Negligible
1860 U.S. War Dept. 10 soldiers firing "as skirmishers"	N.A.	N.A.	N.A.	34%	6%

It would seem that the use of multiple shot offered little advantage over the solid ball. More likely, the use of "goose shot" (for example, John Smith, in Tyler 1907:94) may be attributed to a shortage of musket balls, or the possibility of hunting geese. These tests also raise some doubts regarding Champlain's claim to have shot three Mohawk chiefs at 25 yd in 1609 (Biggar 1922–36:2:99). If the distance was 25 yd, the spread of the shot would have been insufficient to hit more than one chief. If the distance were greater, the projectiles probably would not have been lethal.

While on the subject of lethality, it is interesting to note that while the test muskets loaded with solid ball could penetrate three 2-in. pine boards at 25 yd, two at 75, and at least one at 100, a 0.735 ball, propelled by 125 gr of powder, bounced off of a pine board at 200 yd (albeit, leaving a significant dent). Thus it would seem that the musket was likely to be lethal at a range where there was hope that an individual marksman could hit a single enemy, but may not have been so at longer ranges.

Neither I nor any of my helpers was able to load a musket in a time (from shot A to shot B) of less than 35 seconds. Even this time was achieved only with the aid of a paper cartridge of eighteenth century British design. Using the bandoleer common in the 1600s, with balls in a separate pouch, loading takes at least one minute. This time represents a parade-ground ideal and probably could not be equalled in battle. Needless to say, loading is very difficult if the shooter cannot stand erect.

A bow may be "fired" at least 6 times as rapidly as the gun and may be reloaded when kneeling behind cover. Nor does such a weapon lack range or accuracy. The "self-bow" used by North American Natives had an accurate range of 50–100 yards. Equipped with either Native-made brass or European-made iron arrowheads, it could penetrate armour (Held 1970, Hughes 1974). By the standard of the musket, the bow was incredibly accurate; it is reasonable to assume that experienced bowmen shoot more accurately than even the finest of musketmen. At 20 yd, an Indian bowman "could hit a ten cent piece or a button three times out of five." The Seminole chief, Charlie Snow, "seldom missed a squirrel at twenty yards, often hit at fifty" although he is reported to have missed a wildcat with several arrows at 60 yd. The maximum cast of North American Indian bows appears to have been 90 to 150 yards.

The self-bow should not, of course, be confused with the English longbow which had a cast of 300 yd (French 1954:31–33, Pope 1918). With this latter bow, Victorian archers like H.O. Ford and Maurice Thomson could place 9 of 11 arrows through an 8 in. gourd at 80 yd or place 3 arrows in succession in a 9 and 3/5-in. circle at 100 yd (French 1954:71). Still, the accuracy and range of the self-bow are impressive, and are comparable to those of the musket. Even the 75-year-old Indian bow tested by Saxton Pope could cast an arrow 100 yards. Experiments have shown that flint arrowheads penetrate hide, muscle and bone as well as or better than do arrowheads of steel (French 1954:24, Pope 1918). The bow may be "loaded" in any position, is lighter and (important in guerrilla warfare) is silent.

In addition, the user of the bow is not tied to suppliers outside of his immediate tribal group, where cost and availability are beyond his control. Schlesier (1975:5) is not quite correct in stating that these tools "could be made by everyone in a few minutes without cost and from materials easily available." Arrows tended to be produced by specialist artificers (French 1954:25), perhaps the same individuals who later functioned as gunsmiths (Malone 1973). The important point, however, is that local suppliers within the tribal socio-economic structure could supply weapons and accessories. No manipulative and unreliable outside power could cut off the supply of arrows or refuse to repair bows, as the colonists could with powder, lead, and firearms.

The musket of the seventeenth century had major ergonomic faults, some rectified as early as 1703. These weapons were crudely designed and poorly balanced. While a Queen Anne musket, or its descendent the "Brown Bess," or the French "Charleville" musket "fit" the shooter such that the weapon "shoulders" easily and naturally, the earlier gun does not seem to fit at all (Held 1970), and is front heavy. From my own experience during these tests, I would argue: firstly, that one can learn to shoot an arrow in the general direction of a target as easily as one can shoot a musket ball; and secondly, that to learn to shoot the (sightless) musket accurately is no easier than learning to use a bow. The most perfect of arquebusiers would never be able to equal competent bowmen, due to the limitations of their weapon.

It has been argued that adoption of the matchlock musket in Europe was linked, not to its superiority as a weapon, but to profound economic change (Hughes 1974, French 1954, Wilkinson 1973, Held 1970). The bow required hundreds of hours of practice "while the dullest recruit could learn in a few weeks to shoot a musket." (French 1954:114) Where large standing armies could be trained and maintained, the bow was the best weapon for infantry, but where armies had to be quickly recruited in time of war, the gun was the most effective armament. With the decline of the feudal era the cost of equipping and training standing armies of professional soldiers became prohibitive. The explanation for the universal adoption of the musket for European armies lies less in the realm of technical superiority than in its cost-effectiveness in the European economic context.

In the North American Native context, we might speculate that, once significant numbers of Natives were occupied primarily as traders instead of as hunters and warriors, the cadre of trained bowmen would disappear, or decrease in size. One would argue that as the musket was adopted by those individuals who did not have the time or inclination to become archers, Native use of the gun would have increased with each succeeding generation. As bow-oriented Natives died off or retired they would be succeeded by young men who devoted themselves to trade rather than training for war, and who were therefore better off with muskets. Even so, it is unlikely that such profound socio-economic changes could have taken place during the first few years that firearms were available. Europeans increased inter-tribal trade but they certainly did not introduce it, and there is no evidence to support the notion that proficiency with firearms supplanted skill with bow and arrow among any Native group prior to the introduction of the breech-loading repeating rifle of the nineteenth century.

I have described above the many steps involved in loading the flint musket, and discussed the rates of fire of musket and bow. We know that to compensate for the effect of barrel fouling, arquebusiers used projectiles of such disproportionate diameters to the bores of their pieces that 1/24 to 1/16 in. windage was considered normal. I decided to see if this practice was wholly necessary, reasoning that other factors, such as the need to standardize projectiles such that all guns of a given type could use them despite variance in bore size, might account for this policy. For other reasons too, it was necessary to understand the decrements in utility, however temporary, which would occur during normal use.

The 0.75 cal British musket (no. 6) was used as the test weapon. The gun, having been thoroughly cleaned, was fired repeatedly without cleaning, until it could not be loaded further. The tests were conducted in midsummer during clement weather. I began each test session with new flints and dry powder. Using a 0.730 ball (.02 in. windage) with light cloth patching, loading became difficult after the fifth shot and by the seventh shot the ramrod had to be tapped with a mallet in order to seat the ball on the powder. At this stage of fouling, even an unpatched 0.730 ball could be seated only by repeatedly ramming it with the ramrod. A 0.690 ball (.06 in. windage) on the other hand, loaded with ease even after 20 shots if it was not used with a cloth patch (using instead the British paper "cartouch" of the eighteenth century). With a cloth patch, after 9 or 10 shots the moist sludge lining the barrel caused the ball and patch to stick about 1 ft from the powder. If forced, the ball usually rotated, divesting itself of the patch, then seating easily. When shooting during a damp afternoon with a light drizzle of rain, the problem of barrel fouling was intensified. Although I loaded and shot from under cover, only about 70 percent (15 with 0.69 ball and paper, 7 with the 0.69 ball and cloth, and 3 with 0.730 ball and cloth) of the usual number of shots could be fired before loading became very difficult.

After firing several shots, I allowed the musket to stand without being cleaned for 24 hours. The next day, the coating of relatively dry powder residue inside the bore had absorbed so much moisture that the gun was almost useless. Even thorough field-cleaning could not remove the residue. The weapon was more difficult to load and easily fouled.

After an average of 4 shots the muskets tended to misfire due to the failure of the lock to produce adequate sparks to ignite the primer. At this point, several snaps of the lock were required for ignition of the primer. The problem was caused by a build-up of moist powder residue on the surface of the frizzen and on the flint. Thus lubricated by powder-sludge, the flint produced only a weak spark when it scraped the frizzen. Thorough wiping with a dry cloth usually made 2 or 3 more shots possible before the cleaning had to be repeated (although by this time the flint usually had to be replaced due to wear). In rainy-day conditions, the problem of powder residue was more of a hindrance, and cleaning was necessary after each shot. Even so, the misfire rate was so high that testing had to be discontinued. Of 50 hammer falls, only 11 ignited the priming powder.

A "flash-in-the-pan," however, is of little use by itself. On a dry day, the primer flash usually succeeds in igniting the main charge, but if the humidity is high, the pan becomes damp with powder residue, the touch-hole (communicating between pan and propellant charge) tends to become obstructed, and dampness in the barrel decreases the likelihood of ignition. Of the eleven successful rainy-day primer-ignitions described above, only four ignited the main charge. Further attempts to use flint guns in inclement weather confirmed that a 90 percent misfire rate may not be unusual. I remind the reader that this decrement in reliability was due solely to humidity. I was unable to make the weapon fire reliably when loaded in the open in even a light rain.

In the best weather a 20 to 25 percent misfire rate was normal with good flints if they were replaced every 15 shots. The reliability was improved if new flints were used every 10 shots (modern target shooters use a new flint every six shots). About 80 percent of all misfires were due to the failure of the lock to ignite the primer, while 20 percent were failures of the primer to ignite the propellant charge.

The historical record tends to confirm anecdotally the validity of my estimates of the gun's efficacy. The colonists' guns frequently misfired, and were sensitive to climatic conditions (Trumbull 1846:91–92, Church 1772:123, Bradford and Winslow 1969:51). The gun was so inaccurate that a volley of 50 to 60 musket shots at close range missed Captain Church in 1675 (Church 1772:41–42). Other examples of gunners missing easy targets abound. Nor was the musket consistently effective against body armour (Church 1772:32–33, Bradford and Winslow 1969:52, 55, Gunther 1972).

Many of the casualties attributable to the use of firearms in warfare were caused at close range by the arquebusier's own comrades (for example, Church 1772:58) or by his own weapon blowing up (for example, Bradford and Winslow 1969:38, Schlesier 1975:5–6).

The bow and arrow was accurate and deadly (for example, Biggar 1922–36:3:73–74, Trumbull 1846:90, Covington 1975:23), and could at times pierce even armour (for example, Trigger 1976:360, 417, 418, Latta 1971:127). The gun did not replace the bow; it was simply an addition to the Native arsenal. Perhaps firearms were valued more for their psychological impact. It was not uncommon for Indians to use guns primarily against Natives who were not familiar with their use, and bows against those who had guns (for example, Gooding 1962:27, Kinietz 1965).

The English themselves condemned the gun because it was inaccurate, became hot and dangerous after 8 shots, and blinded shooters with their own smoke. The bow could fire much faster and the psychological effects of a drift of arrows was greater than invisible bullets (French 1954:113).

It is evident that in terms of accuracy, rate of fire, misfire rate, availability and repairablilty, the bow is clearly superior to the musket.

While the maximum range of the musket is greater than that of the bow, its accuracy at long range is atrocious. It could be used effectively only by massed infantry, a configuration which is the antithesis of guerrilla warfare.

Because of its rate of fire, even if we disregard its superior accuracy, the bow is capable of 5 to 12 times the number of hits which are possible with a musket in a given period of time. The bow was more easily obtained, and ammunition supplies were locally available, independent of the Europeans (unless iron arrowheads were used). The bow is lighter and easier to transport than the musket and has the advantages of reliability and silence. Lastly, the bow is more compatible with other weapons such as spears, clubs and hatchets. The arquebusier is loaded down with his heavy weapon, loading tool(s), powder flasks, projectiles (12 to 18 balls weigh 1 lb) and spare flints, and is less able to carry or use other weapons.

Excepting possible psychological or ceremonial utility, it is unlikely that European firearms conferred any advantage whatsoever on Native people. In fact, the bow was a superior weapon. Until the development of breech-loading, and later, repeating rifles, during the nineteenth century, the gun offered no practical advantage over Native weapons.

Chapter Eight

Conclusions and Hypotheses

In the preceding chapters we have examined evidence contrary to the view that European firearms revolutionized Native warfare or became a locus of trade-dependency in the seventeenth century. Weapons such as the true flintlock, which might have been of some use to Native peoples, remained relatively rare until well after 1640, even in the countries in which they were made. All European armies used the matchlock throughout the seventeenth century. Flint guns such as the snaphaunce, Jacobean lock and Miquelet lock, were expensive and much less functional than were the more recently produced weapons familiar to modern collectors.

In Europe, the small-arm was only a single component of a tactical complex that involved extensive use of fortification, heavy ordinance, cavalry and pikemen. Protected by the latter, arquebusiers were used *en masse*. It was not until the eighteenth century that fire-discipline, including rapid-fire techniques and a bayonet, replaced the pikeman and sword. The musket, then, did not act as a primary weapon until after the period under consideration here. Indeed the state of the art of gunmaking was such that the mid-seventeenth century small-arm would probably not have been useful outside of the tactical complex within which the Europeans employed it. Indeed, the arquebus was used in preference to the longbow, not because it was a better weapon, but because it had economic advantages and could be more effective against heavy steel armour.

It seems unlikely that the European settlers were able or inclined to trade large quantities of modern guns to Native people at any time prior to 1675. Because they were outnumbered and intimidated by the peoples whose lands they were occupying, all the colonies prohibited the sale of guns to the Natives. The colonists' supplies of firearms were always sparse and the modern flint guns were not available in sufficient quantities for them to be made mandatory for militia use until quite late in this period. It would appear that few Natives could have acquired arquebuses or would have attempted to do so.

Where guns were acquired by Native peoples, they did not necessarily replace other weapons. Some tribes retained their bows, using guns only against tribes that had none, suggesting that guns were valued more for their psychological than their physical effects. The bow and other Native-made weapons predominated throughout the seventeenth century.

Where Natives used guns there is little evidence that they derived any material advantage from doing so during the first half of the seventeenth century. Hyde (1962:125) argues that when the Iroquois defeated the Eries in 1653, the latter possessed few guns and preferred the bow as a weapon of war. The defeat of the Eries is explained not by Iroquois guns but by their being grossly outnumbered.

The Sioux were initially intimidated by guns, and in 1657 the Tobacco, Hurons and Ottawas were able to cheat and frighten them (Hyde 1962:133). However, though still without guns, by 1670 the Sioux had acquired an appreciation of their weaknesses. Armed only with traditional weapons they were able to drive off and terrorize their oppressors in spite of the guns, French knives and tomahawks possessed by the latter (Hyde 1962:137). If good French flintlocks gave the Tobacco, Huron and Ottawas little advantage over the Sioux in 1670, it seems implausible that a small number of inferior Dutch snaphaunces (if they *were* flint guns) assured Iroquois victory over the Huron in 1648–52. It is evident that firearms did not play a large part in Iroquois attacks during the 1640s either (Hyde 1962:123).

Some tribes that had access to guns thought them to be nonessential. The Ottawas, like most Natives during the first half of the seventeenth century, did not engage in pitched gun battles but discharged an initial volley of projectiles, then proceeded to the attack proper with tomahawks, clubs and knives (Kinietz 1965:254–5). Perrot says that what little advantage the guns gave them was offset by the use of stratagem (Hyde 1962:137). The Eries, as already mentioned, preferred the bow as a weapon (Hyde 1962:125) and only used their guns against tribes that had none. Father Alloues tells us:

> They wage war with 7 or 8 different nations, but do not use guns, finding them too cumbersome and slow. They carry them, never the less, when they march against nations who do not understand the use of them, to frighten them by their noise. (Thwaites 1896–1901:60:161)

The seventeenth century arquebus was only useful as a military weapon in open-field pitched battles involving massed infantry and volley-fire tactics. Even as late as 1846 on the west coast Roderick Finlayson, chief trader at Fort Victoria, tells us that his attempts to impress Natives with musket drill were without effect. A Songhee chief explained the folly of European-style massed infantry tactics compared to the Native practice of fighting from behind cover (Finlayson 1913:17). There is little evidence that any tribe had developed tactics similar to those employed in European battle by the middle of the seventeenth century. This is hardly surprising as the successful use of such tactics requires that they be adopted as a convention by both warring parties. In fact, I have argued (*contra*, Otterbein 1965) that during the early contact period Native tactics changed little to accommodate the firearm.

Finally, I have shown that the Native bow and arrow was a weapon better suited to seventeenth century North American warfare. The gun offers little practical advantage over the bow, while its slow rate of fire, requirement of supplies not locally obtainable, unreliability, difficulty to repair, weight and awkwardness are definite disadvantages. It is probable that the bow could score more hits in a given period of time than could an arquebus.

The Sources of Trade-Dependence

Schlesier (1975) has argued that prior to the Iroquois wars no article of European manufacture offered significant advantages over goods of Native origin. He reminds us that the European trade inventories of the period were very limited and of dubious utility to the Natives. Their main attraction was novelty-value. To the suggestion that iron knives and other edged implements were the stuff of dependency, Schlesier replies:

> . . . stone tools perform, as any archaeologist knows, the same tasks as those made of metal . . . [and] can be resharpened by flaking more quickly than those of metal. Especially, however, stone tools could be made by everyone, in a few minutes, without cost and from materials easily available. (Schlesier 1975:4–5)

In any event, as we have seen, it seems likely that the colonists did not have significant numbers of guns to trade to the Natives. It is not therefore surprising that there is little evidence that any group of Natives had large numbers of guns, or that those they did have were not a significant factor in Native warfare. Further, the gun they could acquire during the 1640s was inferior to the Native bow, and it is apparent that the

Natives recognized this. Where, then, do all these well-armed Natives come from? Four suggestions will be discussed here. First we must question the accuracy of the archival and narrative material on which the ethnohistory of the period is based. Because most of the arms trade was illegal, some scholars argue that such trade was far more extensive than official records suggest. But let us examine our data sources more closely.

The reports to which most authors refer, and which support the idea of extensive weapons trade between 1640 and 1650, were written by individuals for whom this sort of speculation was a life or death matter. All of the colonies had only tenuous footholds in North America during the seventeenth century. Any of them could have been wiped out long before support from Europe could be sought, let alone received. The colonies were surrounded by powerful enemies or potential enemies. These included both the European competitors with whom they had a history of warfare, and the Native populations whose lands and resources they were impinging on and who must, sooner or later, be goaded into military resistance and (most feared of all) inter-tribal unity. It is not surprising that the colonists' fear of each other and of the people whose land they were invading should have become conjoined. Hence, not only were the Natives vilified and feared but slight evidence was taken as proof that they were contemplating attack and were being armed by colonial adversaries.

The New Englanders bemoaned the extensive gun trade of the Dutch and French from whom they were geographically and culturally far removed. The French Jesuits were similarly hostile toward the Puritans and blamed them, not altogether unfairly, for arming their Native enemies (Trigger 1976:628). In fact, all of the European colonies blamed each other for trading arms to the Natives. All, at one time or another, prohibited such trade, and all engaged in it. The English accused the French and Dutch; the Dutch, the Swedes and English; the French, the English and Dutch, and the Swedes everyone else (Burke 1967; Clark 1970; Douglas 1913; Ellis and Morris 1906; Hubbard 1974; Leach 1958; Malone 1973; Mayer 1943; Russell 1957; Snyderman 1948; Trelease 1971; Thomson 1887; Trumbull 1846). We must take into account the fact that our long dead informants were members of populations at risk. The massacre of the Pequot in 1637 (Mather 1972; Mason 1967) and plans for unprovoked attacks in 1642 (Knowles 1934:190–92) are evidence of extreme and sometimes irrational fear. The British humiliation of Alexander and later of his brother Metacomet, which was responsible for King Philip's War of 1675–76, is another example of European sensitivity to potentially hostile Native activity.

As has already been suggested, European fears of Native resistance were not groundless, but the evidence does point to an exaggerated fear on the part of the colonists which may have resulted in gross exaggerations of the Native interest in prosecuting war and, of special interest to us here, of their level and types of armament.

A Social Structural Hypothesis

Kai T. Erikson was interested in other crises and did not discuss the trade in guns to Native people, but his work on the functions of "crisis" may shed light on the issues that interest us here. Erikson offers a social-structural model to explain crises in the Massachusetts Bay Puritan communities. He suggests that, having been originally united largely by persecution in Europe, the New Englanders required either enemies or internal deviance to re-articulate their social boundaries and to create a sense of unity. It is evident that colonial leaders frequently made scapegoats of external enemies, including other European colonists and Native groups, as well as members of their own communities. Erikson describes a series of events during which these same informants discovered heretic Antinomians, demonic Quakers and over 200 witches on their own doorstep; each crisis occurred at times when other indicators tell us that internal stress in the communities had reached a peak (Erikson 1966). The Puritans were not unique in this regard and it is reasonable to suggest that the other colonists also required occasional crises to reinforce unity among their disparate populations. As I have suggested, the English Puritans saw the Jesuits as the embodiment of depravity and found it easy to believe that they would arm the "savages."

Erikson's model, by itself, can explain the colonists' tendency to see a Native behind every tree and a gun in the hands of every Native. It is doubly creditable when we consider the very real, but somewhat vague, risk of ruin. The armed Indian and the villains who equipped him served to give the threat a face and the anxiety it produced a focus.

A Symbolic Interpretation

The newcomers to this continent left cultures that had known the use of guns of one type or another in warfare for over three centuries. Heavy ordinance especially, was capable of terrifying destruction. Loaded with solid ball, cannon could demolish the sturdiest fortification from immense distances (Held 1970, Wilkinson 1973, Hughes 1974). Even the stoutest of men must have paled at the thought of being hit by lead projectiles, some a third of their own weight, which bounced at massed infantry across the battlefield. The big guns were equally horrible when loaded with "canister" (Leblond 1970) and firing hundreds of large musket-balls, their hails of heavy grape shot devastating the ranks at close range. Wall guns, firing one or more balls of 1½ to 3 in. in diameter could demolish a human body at very long range (even Champlain's earliest fortification at Annapolis Royal was equipped with such powerful weapons). Even the heavy hand-held arquebus could be deadly. Firing balls of from 0.80 cal to 1 in. or more in diameter, they were dangerous at 150 to 300 m. These weapons, fired by massed arquebusiers using forked rests to support their weight, were terrifying in aspect and effect (Held 1970, Wilkinson 1973, Hughes 1974). In the context of open-field battle or attacks upon fortifications, the Europeans had ample experience with the awesome destructive power of "villainous saltpetre." It seems likely that the colonists generalized their usually vicarious experience of cannon, wall guns, heavy hand-arms and muskets used in the tactical context of European warfare, to smaller, less effective firearms. These lighter arms had been experienced in the context of massed volley-fire used in combination with other, more destructive weapons. We can hardly blame the colonists for having an exaggerated impression of the destructive potential of the musket. They were surrounded by powerful tribes which could, if united, have easily destroyed them. I would suggest that the colonists needed to develop an image of military superiority to act as a symbol of security. As late as the nineteenth century, European traders on the Northwest Coast were unable to accept that their presence and well-being were insured solely by their usefulness to the Natives and by Native tolerance. As Fisher suggests, the traders' bluster and demonstrations of their weaponry were primarily for their own psychological benefit; they certainly did not impress the Natives (Fisher 1977:15–17, 39–40).

The colonists did in fact have advantages over the Natives in warfare. While the Natives' food supply could be wiped out through raiding, a technique often used, the Europeans' supply was less vulnerable. Provisions could always be received from Europe by ship. Also, while no better armed than the Natives for guerrilla warfare, the colonists had the wherewithal to defend their most important centres against attack. The Europeans had access to the technology of fortification as developed through centuries of siege-warfare in Europe. Indeed, the merit of this technology was recognized by the Natives, who by 1675 had some skilled masons and were building sophisticated forts of their own (Abler 1989:276, Malone 1973:60, Jones 1909:306, Trumbull 1846:72). Heavy ordinance, in combination with fortification, provided a crucial advantage. The earliest colonists equipped themselves with "great guns" and recognized their considerable importance for defence. As early as 1620, Bradford and Winslow reported that the possibility of Native attack "caused us to plant our great ordinances in places most convenient." They had brought ashore four cannons including a "minion" (3–3.5 inch bore and 7–8 feet long) and two "Bases" (1.25-inch bore), a formidable array of artillery for so small a force (Bailey in Bradford and Winslow 1969:81). Any one of these cannon was capable of devastating effect, giving the Europeans a decided defensive advantage which was maintained throughout the period considered here (Peterson 1964). The cannon was such an efficacious weapon that on April 11, 1676 a small group of women was able to hold off an attacking Native war party using an eight pounder cannon, firing "canister" or small shot (Trumbull 1846:87).[1] While Roderick Finlayson tells us that nineteenth century west-coast Natives at Fort McLeod explained to John Tod why the bow and arrow was more effective than the musket (Finlayson 1913:17), Finlayson himself used a cannon in 1843 to destroy an empty Native house with a load of grape shot, thereby persuading the Songhees to negotiate rather than attack (Finlayson 1945:79–80).

The use of heavy ordinance in North America and its impact on Native/European warfare is a matter for a separate study. Suffice it to say that all European colonies possessed cannon and used them effectively for defence (Peterson 1964).

It is likely that to some extent both Native and European perceived the small arm as having most of the attributes of its larger relative. If cannon could be so effective must not "hand cannon" be similarly fearsome? It is also true that small arms could be effective in certain contexts. For these reasons we might suppose that Natives craved the weapons or even deemed them necessary for military survival — until they gained experience with their use in actual combat. Then they would likely eschew the use of firearms as primary military weapons (for example, Fisher 1977:15–17, 39–40), getting along quite well without them (for example, Hyde 1962:134), or use them in a limited way for the psychological effect on themselves (Rowlandson 1962:76) or naive enemies (Gooding 1962:27). Most likely all tribes acquired guns, but used them as an adjunct to aboriginal weapons including the bow (for example, Kinietz 1965).

In view of the Europeans' exaggerated impression of the utility of their own weapons and fear of Natives who possessed them, it is probable that Native desire to acquire guns stemmed in part from their psychological impact on the invaders. Perceiving that the colonists were impressed by Natives who possessed their technology, it is likely that they sought it for the bargaining power it gave them in negotiations as well as possible psychological advantage in battle.

---

[1] The load used here may in fact have been "grape" as opposed to "canister." The latter is a longer range load in which grape shot is loaded into a container, thus ensuring that it will carry farther before scattering.

Deconstruction: History in the Service of the Present

A fourth explanation for the theory of gun-dependent Natives applies in different ways to modern North Americans as well as to our ancestral informants.

Because histories tend to reflect the needs and concerns of both the individuals who created historical records and those analyzing these records, there is a consistent bias in past and many present explanations concerning Native/European interaction during the early contact period. Our historical informants needed to justify their treatment of the Native peoples they came to dominate, and we need to be comfortable with our cultural past and with our economic and social present.

We have discussed some of the reasons why our informants might have exaggerated the Native threat and the state of Native armament. We must also consider the utility of that remembered threat in allowing the chroniclers of that era and their readers to remain comfortable with their recent past and present relationships with the Natives. Since the Natives were portrayed as dangerous and untrustworthy, it could be argued that it was necessary and right to keep them in check. It was necessary, for their own good, to "civilize" them through military action, discriminatory laws and later on through social programs designed to eradicate their culture.

The later concept of Native trade-dependence is a comfortable one for Euro-North Americans. While admitting that non-Native Canadian and American societies have been insensitive to Natives, we can see the resultant destruction of Native societies, in the past and at present, as the unfortunate but inevitable outcome of the interaction between technologically (and we suspect, in other ways) unequal cultures. "It is unfortunate that the Natives could not adapt," we say, "but the loss of their cultures and territories can be seen in an evolutionary perspective wherein the less fit naturally give way to the more advanced." (See Jennings 1975 for supporting examples.) This view contrasts with the far less comfortable Native view that their ancestors were conquered through a combination of competition, trickery and brutality, and that their later trade-dependence resulted from being deprived of both the human and natural resources required for survival.

This generation of North Americans seems intent, however, upon recognizing the multiple truths and, at least at the level of public ritual, redressing some of the injustices of our recent history. We have begun to re-examine the European colonization of North America and revise our understanding of the cultural heritage of the original peoples who were so often overwhelmed by it. I hope that the present work contributes, in some small way, to that process.

Appendix

Notes on Lethality

Regrettably, the many factors which combine to increase the likelihood that a given firearm will kill, or more importantly, stop an adversary, cannot be incorporated in a single formula. We can, however, calculate a projectile's kinetic energy; the capacity of the projectile to do work at point of impact can be used as a correlate of the ability of a projectile to incapacitate a human being, or its "stopping power." Because kinetic energy figures are meaningless without a basis for comparison, I present data for a modern military rifle as well as for one of the muskets referred to in Chapter Four. The weapons for which the following calculations were made are the 0.75 cal Short Land Pattern musket, and the 0.308 N.A.T.O. cartridge used until recently by the Canadian Armed Forces. The musket fires a 0.715 cal ball weighing 545 gr while the 0.30 cal N.A.T.O. cartridge uses a 150 gr projectile.

Distance (yd)	Military Musket (ft-lb.)	Modern Military Rifle (ft-lb.)
At muzzle	847 (@ 800 fps)	2,700 (@ 2,800 fps)
50	706	2,500
100	593 (@ 669 fps)	2,200 (@ 2,500 fps)
150	499,	
200	420	1,800
300	297 (@ 473 fps)	1,500 (@ 2,000 fps)

Note: fps = feet per second.

It is clear from these figures that the modern weapon is at least three times as powerful as the musket at close range. This superiority increases to a factor of five at 300 yards. Naturally, other factors such as the behaviour on impact (penetration, expansion, etc.) of the round ball or elongated bullet have to be taken into account. However, it is obvious that the musket fares badly in this sort of comparison.

Bibliography

Abler, Thomas S. (1989) "European Technology and the Art of War in Iroquoia," in *Proceedings of the 20th Conference of the University of Calgary Archaeological Association*. Edited by D.C. Tkaczuk and B.C. Vivian. Calgary: Calgary Archaeological Association.

Assembly, General of Virginia (1915) "Acts, Orders and Resolutions of the General Assembly of Virginia: at Sessions of March 1643–1646," *Virginia Magazine of History and Biography*. Vol. 23, July 5, 1915:225–255.

Baird, Donald "A Ketland Pistol for the American Indian Trade," *The Canadian Journal of Arms Collecting*. 12:2:39–42.

Balikci, Asen (1964) *Development of Basic Socio-Economic Units In Two Eskimo Communities*. (Bulletin #202). Ottawa: National Museum of Canada, Anthropological Series, No. 69.

Bartlett, John R. (1856–65) *Records of the Colony of Rhode Island and Providence Plantation In New England*. 10 vols. Providence: A.C. Green, State Printers. Also available in reprint, New York: AMS Press, 1968.

Beckham, Stephen Dow (1971) *Requiem For A People*. Norman: University of Oklahoma Press.

Bernard, L.L. (1944) *War and its Causes*. New York: Henry Holt & Co.

Biggar, H.P. (ed.) (1922–36) *The Memoires of Samuel de Champlain*. 6 vols. Toronto: Champlain Society.

Bonfanti, Leo (1971) *The Pequot-Mohican War*. Wakefield: Pride Pub. Inc.

Boone, Nicholas (1701) *Military Discipline*. Boston.

Bouchard, Russel (1977) "The Trade Gun In New France 1690–1760." *The Canadian Journal of Arms Collecting*. 15:1:3–12.

Bouton, N. and others (1867–1941) *New Hampshire Provincial and State Papers*. 40 vols. Concord, N.H.: E.A. Jenks, State Printer. Also available in reprint, New York: AMS Press.

Bradford, William (1952, 1856) *Of Plymouth Plantation 1620–1647*. Reprint (original published Boston: 1856 with the title *History of Plymouth Plantation*). New York: Knopf.

Bradford, William and Winslow, Edward (1969, 1622) *Mourt's Relation or Journal of the Plantation at Plymouth*. Reprint (original John Bellamie 1622). New York: Garret Press.

Bradley, James W. (1987) *Evolution of the Onondaga Iroquois: Accommodating Change 1500–1655*. Syracuse: Syracuse University Press.

Bridges, Toby (ed.) (1972) "Care, Cleaning & Black Powder," in *Black Powder Gun Digest*. Northfield: Digest Books Inc.

———— (1972) "Firepower Along the Mason Dixon," in *Black Powder Gun Digest*. Northfield: Digest Books Inc.

Brown, Alexander (1890, 1897) *The Genesis of the United States*. 2 vols. Boston.

———— (1969) *The First Republic In America*. Reprint (1898 original). New York: Russell and Russell.

Brown, M. L. (1971) "Early Gun Makers Met War Woes," *The American Rifleman*. 119:92–97.

Brown, M. L. (1978) "Matchlocks in Spanish Florida." in *Gun Digest*. Edited by John T. Amber. Northfield: D.B.I. Books Inc.

Brown, M. L. (1976) "Firearms in Frontier America—The Economic Impact. Part I –1560 to 1800." in *Gun Digest*. Edited by John T. Amber. Chigago: Follet Pub. Co.

Brown, William H. (*et al.*, eds.) (1828–1912) *Archives of Maryland*. 72 vols. Baltimore: Maryland Historical Society.

Burke, Charles T. (1967) *Puritans at Bay: The War Against King Philip and the Squaw Sachems in new England 1675–1676*. New York: Exposition Press.

Caldwell, Warren W. (1960) "Comments of The "English Pattern" Trade Rifle." *Missouri Archaeologist*. 22:50–62.

Cheever, George B. (1848) *The Journal of the Pilgrims at Plymouth in New England, in 1620*. New York: John Wiley.

Chown, John (1976–77) National War Museum, personal communications.

Church, Thomas (1845) *The History of the Great Indian War of 1675 and 1676, Commonly called Philip's War*. Boston 1716, 1st ed., (third edition edited by Samuel G. Drake) New York: Dayton.

Church, Thomas (1772) *The Entertaining History of King Philip's War* (first edition, Boston, 1716). Newport.

Clark, Charles E. (1970) *The Eastern Frontier: the Settlement of Northern New England 1610–1763*. New York: Alfred A. Knopf.

Clifford, James and Marcus, G. E. (1986) *Writing Culture: the Poetics and Politics of Ethnography*. Berkeley: University of California Press.

Cohn, John (1975) *Europe's Inner Demons*. Frogmore: Grenada Pub. Ltd.

Colden, Cadwallader (1958) *The History of the Five Indian Nations: Depending on the Province of New York in America*. New York: Ithaca.

Coles, John (1973) *Archaeology By Experiment*. London: Hutchinson University Library.

Cook, Sherburne F. (1973) "Interracial Warfare and Population Decline Among the New England Indians," *Ethnohistory*:20:1–24.

Copeway, G. (1850) *The Traditional History and Characteristic Sketches of the Ojibway Nation*. London: Charles Gilpin.

Cotterman, D. (1972) "Harnessing The Powder Demon," in *Black Powder Gun Digest*. Edited by Toby Bridges. Northfield: Digest Books Inc.

Covington, James W. (1975) "Relations between the Eastern Timucuan Indians and the French and Spanish 1564–1567," in *Four Centuries of Southern Indians*. Edited by Charles M. Hudson. Athens: University of Georgia Press.

Darling, Anthony D. (1970) *Red Coat and Brown Bess*. Ottawa: Museum Restoration Service.

Darling, Anthony D. (1971) "The Combination Matchlock and Wheel lock: The Montecuccoli System." *The Canadian Journal of Arms Collecting*. 9:3:92–97.

Davis, William T. (1964) *Bradford's History of Plymouth Plantation 1606–1646*. Reprint. New York: Barnes & Noble.

De Vries, Daniel (1857) *Short Historical and Journal Notes*. Reprint (Alkmeer 1655). New York: New York Historical Society.

Dean, J. (1946) *Deane's Manual of the History and Science of Fire Arms*. Reprint (original 1858). Huntington: Standard Publications.

Dexter, H.M. (1905) *The England and Holland of the Pilgrims*. Cambridge: The Riverside Press.

Dolomieu, Citizen (1960) "Report on the Art of Making Gunflints (Fire-Flint)" (Original written by Citizen Dolomieu in the Year 5) *Missouri Archaeologist*. 22:50–61.

Douglas, James (1913) *New England and New France*. Toronto: William Briggs.

Downing, Emmanuel (1910) "Letter from Emmanuel Downing to James Usher, 1620." *Collections of the Massachusetts Historical Society*. (Fourth Series). New York: Charles Scribner's Sons.

Drake, Samuel G. (1975) *Indian Captivities, or Life in the Wigwam*. Reprint (1851 original). New York: AMS Press.

——— (1976) *The Old Indian Chronicle*. Reprint (1867 original). New York: AMS Press.

Du Mont, John S. (1977) *Custer Battle Guns*. Highland Park: The Gunroom Press.

Dunning, R.W. (1959) *Social and Economic Change Among the Northern Ojibwa*. Toronto: University of Toronto Press.

Eckert, Allan W. (1970) *The Conquerors*. Boston: Little, Brown and Co.

Edsall, James (1975) *The Story of Firearms Ignition*. Union City: Pioneer Press.

Egles, Ross (1976) "Canadian Indian Treaty Guns," *The Canadian Journal of Arms Collecting*. 14:2:53–60.

Ellis, George W. and Morris, John E. (1906) *King Philip's War*. New York: Grafton Press.

Embree, Edwin R. (1970, 1973) *Indians of the Americas*. Reprint (1939 original). 2 vols. New York: Collier Books.

Erikson, Kai T. (1966) *Wayward Puritans—A Study in the Sociology of Deviance*. New York: John Wiley & Sons Inc.

Fernow, Berthold (1897) "Minutes of the Court of Burgomasters And Schepens 1653–55" *The Records of New Amsterdam*. Vol 1. New York: The Knickerbocker Press.

Finlayson, Roderick (1913) *Biography of Roderick Finlayson*. Victoria. Filmed from a copy of the original publicaiton held by the Library Division, Provincial Archives of British Columbia. Ottawa: Canadian Institute for Historical Microreproductions.

———— (1945) *History of Vancouver Island and the Northwest Coast*. Saint Louis: Saint Louis University Press.

Fisher, Robin (1977) *Contact and Conflict: Indian-European Relations in British Columbia, 1774-1890*. Vancouver: University of British Columbia Press.

Ford, Worthington C. (1968) *Journals of the Continental Congress, 1774–1789*. 34 vols. Reprint. New York: Johnson Reprint Corp.

Foreman, Grant (1953) *Indian Removal: The Emigration of the Five Civilized Tribes Advancing the Frontiers, 1830–1860*. Norman: University of Oklahoma Press.

Franklin, J. (1937) *Narratives of New Netherlands, 1609–1664*. New York: Barnes and Noble.

French, Charles Chenevix (1954) *A History of Marksmanship*. Chicago: Follet Pub. Co.

Fuller, Claud E. (1958) *The Rifled Musket*. New York: Bonanza Books.

Furst, Bob (1972) "Two Centuries of Black Powder," in *Black Powder Gun Digest*. Edited by Toby Bridges. Northfield: Digest Books Inc.

Gaier, Claude (1976) *Four Centuries of Siege Gunmaking*. London: Sotheby/Park Bennet.

Gendron, Francis (1868) *Quelques particularitez du pay des Hurons en la Nouvelle France remarquest par le Sieur Gendron, docteur en medecine qui a demeuré dans ce pays—la fort longtemps*. New York: J. Munsell.

Gibson, Charles (1966) *Spain In America*. New York: Harper Torchbooks.

Gillet-Laumont, F.P.N. (1960) "Extract From a Report By Citizen Salivet On the Making of Gunflints in the Departments of Indre and Loiret-Cher," *Missouri Archaeologist*. 22:62-70.

Given, Brian J. (1989) "Contemporary Ethnohistory: Rethinking Trade Dependence," in *A Different Drummer: Readings in Anthropology With A Canadian Perspective*. Edited by Bruce Cox, Jacques Chevalier and Valda Blundell. Ottawa: Carleton U. Press.

Goldstein, R. (1969) *French Iroquois Diplomatic and Military Relations 1609–1701*. The Hague: Mouton & Co.

Gooding, S. James (1976) "Trade Guns of the Hudson's Bay Company 1670 to 1700." *The Canadian Journal of Arms Collecting*. 13:3.

——— (1974) *The Gunsmiths of Canada Historical Arms Series No. 14*. Ottawa: Museum Restoration Service.

——— (1962) *The Canadian Gunsmiths 1608 to 1900*. West Hill, Ontario: Museum Restoration Service.

——— (1960) "A Preliminary of the Trade Guns Sold By the Hudson's Bay Company," *Missouri Archaeologist*. 22:81–95.

Goodman, Hank (1975) *Muzzle Loader's Manual*. Hawthorne: Ultra-Hi Products Co. Inc.

Gookin, Daniel (1972) *An Historical Account of the Doing and Sufferings of the Christian Indians in New England in the Years 1675, 1676, 1677*. Reprint (#24362). New York: Arno Press.

Gordon, Robert B. (1959) "Early Gunsmith's Metals," *The American Rifleman* 107:12.

Greener, W.W. (1986) *The Gun and its Development*. (reprint of 1910 edition. Original: 1881, London: Cassel & Co.). London: Arms and Armour Press.

Griffin, James B. (1961) *Lake Superior Copper and the Indians*. (Anthropological papers #17). Ann Arbor: Museum of Anthropology, University of Michigan.

Gunther, Erna. (1972) *Indian Life on the Northwest Coast of North America*. Chicago: University of Chicago Press.

Hadlock, Wendell S. (1947) "War Among the Northeastern Woodland Indians," *American Anthropologist*. 49:204–221.

Hagerty, Gilbert W. (1985) *Wampum, War and Trade Goods West of the Hudson*. Interlaken, N.Y: Heart of the Lakes Publishing.

Hamilton, Edward P. (1972) *Native American Bows*. New York: George Shumway.

——— (1967) *The French Army In America and the Musketry Drill of 1755*. Ottawa: Museum Restoration Service (Historical Arms Series #7).

——— (1968) *Early Indian Trade Guns 1625–1775*. Contributions to the Museum of the Great Plains, #3. Lawton, Oklahoma.

——— (1960) "Some Gun Parts From 17th Century Seneca Sites," *Missouri Archaeologist*. 22:99–114.

Hamilton, T.M. (1960) "The Determination of Date and Origin of Archaeological Gun Parts," *Missouri Archaeologist*. 22:5–16.

——— (1960) "Additional Comments on Gunflints," *Missouri Archaeologist*. 22:74–79.

——— (1960) "Concluding Comments and Observations," *Missouri Archaeologist*. 22:206–208.

Hanson, Charles E. Jr. (1961) "An Indian Trade Gun of 1680," *Missouri Archaeologist*. 22:96–8.

Held, Robert (1970) *The Age of Firearms*. Northfield: Gun Digest Co.

Hening, William W. (1971) *Statutes at Large: Being a Collection of all the Laws of Virginia*. 13 Vols. Richmond: Virginia State Library.

Hoadly, Charles J. (1850–1890) *The Public Records of the Colony of Connecticut*. 15 vols. Hartford: Press of the Case, Lockwood & Brainard Co.

Hubbard, William (1974) *Narrative of the Troubles With the Indians.* Reprint, revised by Samuel Drake (1677 original under the title, *The History of the Indian Wars in New England*). London: Arms and Armour Press. Also available in reprint under the title *Narrative of the Indian Wars in New England*. New York: B. Franklin (1971).

Hughes, Maj. Gen. (1974) *Firepower.* London: Arms and Armour Press.

Hunt, G. (1972) *The Wars of the Iroquois.* Madison: University of Wisconsin Press.

Huntington, R.T. (1960) "Identification of Unmarked Gunlocks," *Missouri Archaeologist.* 22:16–25.

Hyde, George E. (1962) *Indians of the Woodlands From Prehistoric Times to 1725.* Norman: University of Oklahoma Press.

Jameson, J.F. (1959) *Narratives of New Netherland 1609–1664.* Reprint. New York: Barnes and Noble.

Jennings, Francis (1975) *The Invasion of America—Indians, Colonialism and the Cant of Conquest.* Chapel Hill: University of North Carolina Press.

Jogues, Father Isaac (1973) "Captivity of Father Isaac Jogues of the Society of Jesus Among the Mohawks," (1642) in *Held Captive By Indians.* Edited by Van Der Beets. Knoxville: University of Tennessee Press.

———— (1973) "Letter from Rensselaerwyck, Aug. 5, 1643," in *Held Captive By Indians.* Edited by Van Der Beets. Knoxville: University of Tennessee Press.

Jones, Arthur E. (1909) *"Wendake Ehen" or Old Huronia.* (Fifth Report of the Bureau of Archives for the Province of Ontario). Toronto: Kings Printer.

Joselyn, John (1988) *Account of Two Voyages to New England.* Reprint (1675 original). Hanover: University Press of New England.

Keegan, John (1976) *The Face of Battle.* New York: Viking Press.

Kellogg, Louise Phelps (1925) *The French Regime in Wisconsin and the Northwest.* Madison: State Historical Society of Wisconsin.

Kennett, Lee (1978) "Gun Proof in Belgium," in *Gun Digest*. Edited by John T. Amber. Northfield: D.B.I. Books Inc.

Kidd, Kenneth E. (1949) *The Excavation of Ste Marie I*. Toronto: University of Toronto Press.

Kinietz, W. Vernon (1965)*The Indians of the Western Great Lakes 1615–1760*. Ann Arbor: Univ. of Michigan Press (Ann Arbor Paperbacks).

Kirkland, Turner (1972) "Loading and Shooting Black Powder Guns," *Black Powder Gun Digest*. Edited by T. Bridges. Northfield: Digest Books Inc.

Kist, J.B., Van Der. Sloot, R.B., Puype, J.P., Van Der Mark, W. (1974) *Niederlandische Musketen und Pistolen*. Akademische Druck—U. Verlagsanstalt Graz.

Knowles, James D. (1934) *Memoir of Roger Williams, the Founder of the State of Rhode Island*. Boston: Lincoln, Edmonds and Co.

La Hontan, Baron de. (1970) *New Voyages to North America*. Reprint (of English edition of 1703) 2 vols. Edited by R.G. Thwaites. New York: B. Franklin.

Latta, M.A. "Archaeology of the Pentang Peninsula," in *Palaeoecology and Ontario Prehistory II*, DAUTRR, No. 2:116–36.

Lauerma, Matti (1956) *L'artillerie de campagne francaise pendant les guerres de la Révolution: évolution de l'organisation et de la tactique*. Helsinki: Heshushirjapino.

Leblonde (1970) *A Treatise of Artillery*. (the first Part of Le Blonde's Elements of War). Generic Title: Éléments de la guerre des sièges. Ottawa: Museum Restoration Service. (original 1743).

Leach, Douglas Edward (1958) *Flintlock and Tomahawk: New England in King Philip's War*. New York: Macmillan Company.

Levermore, Charles H. (1912) *Forerunners and Competitors of the Pilgrims and Puritans*. 2 vols. Brooklyn, New York: New England Society of Brooklyn.

Levett, Christopher (1843) *A Voyage into New England, begun in 1623 and ended in 1624 performed by Christopher Levett*. Collections of the Massachusetts Historical Society. 3:8:159–191. Boston: Little Brown.

Lincoln, Charles H. (1966) *King Philip's War Narratives*. Ann Arbor, University Microfilms Inc. 1966.

——— (1941) *Narratives of the Indian Wars 1675–1699*. Reprint. New York: Barnes & Noble.

Lindquist, G.E.E. (1973) *The Red Man In the United States*. Reprint. New York: George H. Doran, Co.

Lindsey, Merril (1975) *The New England Gun—The First Two Hundred Years*. New York: The David Mckay Co.

Lisiansky, Vrey (1814) *Voyage Round the World in the Years 1803,4,5,6*. London.

Long, J. (1971) *Voyages And Travels of an Indian Interpreter And Trader*. Reprint. Toronto: Coles Publishing.

Lostelneau, Sieur de. (1649) *Le Marexhal de Bataille*. Paris.

Lubbock, John (1870) *The Origin of Civilization and the Primitive Condition of Man; Mental and Social Conditions of Savages*. London: Longman's Green.

Lugs, Jaroslav (1973) *Firearms Past and Present*. 2 vols. London: Greenville Publishing.

Malone, Patrick M. (1991) *The Skulking Way of War: Technology and Tactics Among the New England Indians*. New York: Madison Books.

——— (1973) "Changing Military Technology Among the Indians of Southern New England 1600–1677," *American Quarterly*. 25:56–8.

——— (1971) *Indian and English Military Systems in New England in the Seventeenth Century*. Dissertation, Brown University.

Markham, Gervase (1968) *The Art of Archerie*. Reprint. London: Arms and Armour Press.

Mason, Maj. John (1967) *A Brief History of the Peqout War ... In 1637: Written by Major John Mason, A Principle Actor Therein, as then Chief ...* (National Museum of Canada Anthropology Paper #13). Ottawa: Queen's Printer.

Mason, Otis Tufton (1894) *Woman's Share In Primitive Culture*. New York: Appleton.

Mather, Cotton (1972) *Magnalia Christi Americana*. New York: Arno Press.

Mather, Increase (1676) *A Brief History of the War with the Indians of New England*. Plymouth: John Foster.

———— (1972) *A Relation of the Troubles which have happened in New England by Reason of the Indians There, from the Year 1614 to the Year 1675*. Reprint. (original Boston: John Foster, 1677). New York: Arno Press Inc.

Mayer, Joseph R. (1943) *Flintlocks of the Iroquois 1620–1687*. (Research Records of the Rochester Museum of Arts and Sciences No. 6). New York: Rochester Museum of Arts and Sciences.

Miers, Earl Schenck (1964) *Where the Raritan Flows*. New Brunswick, N.J: Rutgers University Press.

Miller, Perry (1939) *The New England Mind: The Seventeenth Century*. New York: Macmillan.

Morgan, Lewis Henry (1962) *League of the Iroquois*. New York: Corinth Books.

Morman A.U.B. and Pottingen D. (1966) *A History of War and Weapons*. New York: Thomas Y. Crowell Co.

Morton, Nathaniel (1937) *New England's Memorial, Plymouth 1669*. Edited by Howard J. Hall. New York: Scholars Facsimiles & Reprints.

Morton, Thomas (1972) *New English Canaan (or) New Canaan*. Reprint (1637 original). New York: Arno Press.

Muller, William (1811) *The Elements of the science of war: containing the modern, established, and approved principles of the theory and practice of the military sciences*. London: Longman, Hurst, Rees and Orme.

Myers, A.C. (1959) *Narratives of Early Pennsylvania, West New Jersey and Delaware 1630–1707*. New York: Barnes and Noble.

Nelson, Richard K. (1973) *Hunters of the Northern Forest*. Chicago: University Of Chicago Press.

Nonte, Maj. George C. Jr. (1976) *Black Powder Guide*. New Jersey: Stoeger Publishing Co.

O'Callaghan, E.B. (1853–87) *Documents Relating to the Colonial History of the State of New York; procured in Holland, England and France by John Romeyn Brodhead*. 15 vols. Albany: Weed, Parsons & Co.

——— (1849–51) *The Documentary History of the State of New York*. 4 vols. Albany: Weed, Parsons & Co.

O'Donnell, James H. (1975) "The Southern Indians in the War for American Independence, 1775–1783," in *Four Centuries of Southern Indians*. Edited by Charles Hudson. Athens: University of Georgia.

Osgoode, H. (1904–07) *The American Colonies In the Seventeenth Century*. 3 vols. New York: The MacMillan Company.

Otterbein, K. (1970) *The Evolution of War: A Cross-Cultural Study*. New York: HRAF Press.

Otterbein, K. (1965) "Why the Iroquois Won—An Analysis of Military Tactics," *Ethnohistory*. 2:56-63.

Palfrey, John Gorham (1858) *History of New England*. Boston: Little Brown & Co.

Palmer, William P. and Flournoy, H.W. (1968) *Calendar of Virginia State Papers and Other Manuscripts*. 11 vols. Reprint (original 1875–93). New York: Kraus Reprint Corporation.

Parkman, F. (1867) *The Jesuits in North America In The Seventeenth Century*. Boston: Little Brown & Co.

Patterson, E. Palmer (1972) *The Canadian Indian: A History Since 1500*. Don Mills: Collier-Macmillan Canada Ltd.

Paquin, Julien (1932) *The Tragedy of Old Huronia (Wendake ehen) by a pilgrim; a popular story of the Jesuit Huron missions of Canada 1615–1650*. Fort Ste. Marie: The Martyr's Shrine.

Pendergast, James F. (1966) *Three Prehistoric Iroquois Components In Eastern Ontario: The Salem, Gray's Creek and Beckstead Sites* (National Museum of Canada, Bulletin #208, Anthropology Series #73). Ottawa: Department of the Secretary of State.

Percy, George (1922) "A Trewe Ralaycon," *Tyler's Quarterly Historical and Genealogical Magazine*. vol.III: April:264.

Peterson, Harold L. (1956) *Arms and Armour in Colonial America 1526–1783*. Harrisburg: The Stackpole Co.

Peterson, Harold L. (1964) *Encyclopedia of Firearms*. London: The Connoisseur Press.

Pollard, Maj. H.B.C. (1973) *A History of Firearms*. New York: Burt Franklin.

Pope, Saxton T. (1918) *Yahi Archery*. Berkeley: University of California Press.

———— (1923) *A Study of Bows and Arrows*. Berkeley: University of California Press.

Pratt, Peter P. (1976) *Archaeology of the Oneeida Iroquois* (Vol. 1. Occasional Publications in Northeastern Anthropology). George's Mills, New Hampshire: Man in the Northeast Inc.

Preston, Richard, Wise, Sydney and Werner, Herman (1968) *Men in Arms*. New York: Praeger.

Pritts, Joseph (1977) *Incidents of Border Life*. Reprint. (original 1839 Chambersburg Pa: J. Pritts) New York: Garland Publishing Co.

Puype, Jan Piet (1985) *Dutch and Other Flintlocks from Seventeenth Century Iroquois Sites*. (Part I, Proceedings of the 1984 Trade Gun Conference, Research Records #18) New York: Rochester Museum & Science Center.

Quain, Buell H. (1961) "The Iroquois" in *Cooperation and Competition Among Primitive Peoples*. Edited by Margaret Mead. Boston: Beacon Press, 240–81.

Quimby, George (1966) *Indian Culture and European Trade Goods*. Westport: Greenwood Press.

Quimby, George (1960) *Indian Life on the Upper Great Lakes*. Madison: University of Wisconsin Press.

R & E Associates (1970) *1609–1909 The Dutch in New Netherland and the United States*. Reprint (original 1909). San Francisco: R & E Research Assoc.

Ramage, C. Kenneth (1975) *Black Powder Basics, Lyman Product for Shooters*. Middlefield: Lyman Gun Sight Corp.

———— (1975) *Lyman Black Powder Handbook*. Middlefield: Lyman Gun Sight Corp.

———— (1973) *Lyman Cast Bullet Handbook.* Middlefield: Lyman Gun Sight Corp.

———— (1964) *Lyman Reloading Handbook* Middlefield: Lyman Gun Sight Corp.

Ray, Arthur J. (1974) *Indians in the Fur Trade: Their Role as Trappers, Hunters, Middlemen in the Lands Southwest of Hudson Bay, 1660–1870.* Toronto: University of Toronto Press.

Ray, Dorothy Jean (1992) *The Eskimo of the Bering Strait 1650–1898.* Seattle: University of Washington Press.

Richter, Daniel K. (1983) "War and Culture: The Iroquois Experience," *William and Mary Quarterly.* (3rd Series) 40:528–559.

Rowlandson, Mary (1962) *The Sovereignty and Goodness of God, Together with the Faithfulness of his Promises Displayed.* Reprint (1676 original). Berkely: University of California Press.

Russell, Carl P. (1957) *Guns on the Early Frontiers: A History of Firearms from Colonial Times Through the Years of the Western Fur Trade.* Berkely: University of California Press.

Ruttenbur, E.M. (1971) *History of the Indian Tribes of Hudson's River.* Port Washington, N.Y.: I. J. Friedman Division, Kennikat Press.

Saint Remy, Le Surirey de. (1940) *Memoirs D'Artillerie.* Mt. Vernon, New York: Captain James E. Hicks.

Saltonstal, Nathaniel (1966) "The Present State of Newe England With Respect to the Indian War," *King Philip's War Narratives.* Ann Arbor: Ann Arbor University Microfilm. Inc.

Scheele, Raymond (1950) *Warfare of the Iroquois and Their Northern Neighbours.* (Unpublished Dissertation). New York: Columbia University.

Schellenberg, James A. (1982) *The Science of Conflict.* New York: Oxford University Press.

Schlesier, K. (1975) "Die Irokesenkriege und die Grosse Vertreibung, 1609–1656," *Zeitschrift fur Ethnologie.* Braunschweig:100.

————(1976) "Epidemics, European Trade Goods and Indian Middlemen." Paper presented at the annual meetings of the American Society for Ethnohistory, Albuquerque.

Service, Elman R. (1954) *Spanish-Guarani Relations in Early Colonial Paraguay.* Ann Arbor: University of Michigan Press.

Shurtleff, Nathaniel B. (1853–54) *Records of the Governor and Company of Massachusetts Bay in New England.* 5 vols. Boston: W. White.

Shurtleff, Nathaniel B. and Pulsifer, D. (1855–1861) *Records of the Colony of New Plymouth In New England.* 12 vols. Boston. W. White.

Singer, J. David and Associates (1979) *Explaining War: Selected Papers From the Correlates of War Project.* London: Sage Publications.

Smith, Capt. John (1907) "A True Relation of Maryland," in *Narratives of Early Virginia 1606–1625.* Edited by L.G. Tyler. New York: Barnes and Noble.

———— (1970) *General History of Virginia, New England, and the Summer Isles.* Reprint (original 1624). Indianapolis: Bobbs-Merill.

———— (1616) *Description of New England: or the observations and discources of Captain John Smith (admirall of that country) in the north of America, in the year of our Lord 1614; with the successe of sixe ships, that went the year 1615; and the accidents befell him among the French men of warre: with the proofe of the present benefit this country affords; whither this present yeare, 1616, eight voluntary ships are gone to make further tryall.* London: H. Lownes. Also published in reprint with the title *Description of New England.* Washington: P. Force, 1837.

———— (1631) *Advertisements for the Unexperienced Planter in New-England or any where; or, The path-way to experience to erect a plantation.* London: J. Haviland. Also published in photoreprint with the title *Advertisements for the planters of New-England.* New York: Da Capo Press, 1971.

Smith, Carlyle S. (1960) "Experiments in Checking Documented Dates Against Dates Derived from Trade Goods," *Missouri Archaeologist.* 22:25–7.

———— (1960) "Two 18th Century Reports on the Manufacture of Gunflints in France," *Missouri Archaeologist.* 22:40–49.

Snyderman, George S. (1979) *Behind the Tree of Peace: A Sociological Analysis of Iroquois Warfare.* Reprint (of author's thesis, University of Pennsylvania, 1948). New York: AMS Press.

Stoddart, Francis R. (1973) *The Truth About The Pilgrims*. Baltimore: Genealogical Publishing Co. Inc.

Strachey, William (1612) *For the Colony in Virginea Brittania: Lawes, Divine, Morall and Martiall*. London: W. Burre.

Thomson, John Lewis (1887) *History of the Indian Wars and War of the Revolution of the United States*. Philadelphia: J.B. Lippincott Co.

Thwaites, Reuben (1896–1901) *The Jesuit Relations and Allied Documents*. New York: Burrows Bros. Co.

Tooker, Elizabeth (1963) "The Iroquois Defeat of the Huron: A Review of Causes," *Pennsylvania Archeologist*. 33:115–123.

Trelease, Allen W. (1971) *Indian Affairs in Colonial New York: The Seventeenth Century*. (ca. 1960). Port Washington: Ira J. Friedman Division, Kennikat Press.

——— (1962) "The Iroquois and the Western Fur Trade: A Problem in Interpretation," *The Mississippi Valley Historical Review*. 49:32–51.

Trigger, Bruce G. (1985) *Natives and Newcomers: Canada's Heroic Age Reconsidered*. Toronto: University of Toronto Press.

——— (1975) "Brecht and Ethnohistory," *Ethnohistory*. 22:51–56.

——— (1976) *The Children of Uataentsic: A History of the Huron People to 1660*. Toronto: McGill-Queens.

——— (1971) "Champlain Judged by His Indian Policy: A Different View of Early Canadian History," in *Pilot Not Commander*. Edited by Lotz, P.&J. *Anthropologica* N.S.:13:1 & 2:85–114.

——— (1969) *The Impact of Europeans on Huronia*. Toronto: Copp Clark.

——— (1969) *The Huron: Farmers of the North*. New York: Holt, Rinehart and Winston.

Trumbull, Benjamin (1848) *A General History of New England, From the Discovery to MDCLXXX*. (Series 2, vols. 5, 6) Reprint (original 1815). Boston: Massachusetts Historical Society Collections.

——— (1846) *History of the Indian Wars: to Which is Prefixed a Short Account the Discovery of America by Columbus and of the Land*. Boston: Phillips and Sampson.

———— (1818) *A Complete History of Connecticut 1630–1764 and to the close of the Indian Wars*. 2 vols. New Haven: Maltby, Goldsmith & Co. Also available in reprint, New York: Arno Press, 1972.

Tyler, L.G. (1907) *Narratives of Early Virginia 1606–1625*. New York: Barnes and Noble.

Une, Andrew, M.D. (1846) *A Dictionary of Arts, Manufactures and Mines: Containing A Clear Exposition of their Principles and Practice*. London: Longman, Brown, Green and Longmans.

Upper Canada Historical Arms Society (1963) *The Military Arms of Canada* (Historical Arms Series #1). Ottawa: Museum Restoration Service.

Van der Donck, Adriaen (1800, 1841) *A Description of the New Netherlands*. (2nd series. Reprint of 1638 and 1656 publications respectively) in *New York Historical Society Collections*. Edited by Jeremiah Johnson. New York: New York Historical Society.

Van Der Beets, Richard (1973) *Held Captive By Indians—Selected Narratives 1642–1836*. Knoxville: University of Tennessee Press.

Van Laer, Arnold J.F. (1974) *New Netherland Council, Council Minutes*. translated and annotated by Arnold Van Laer. Baltimore: Geneological Publishing Company.

Ward, Harry M. (1961) *The Unitied Colonies of New England*. New York: Vantage Press.

Weber, Eugene (1972) *The Western Tradition*. Lexington: D.C. Heath and Co.

Wedel, Mildred Mott (1974) "Le Sueur and the Dakota Sioux," in *Aspects of Upper Great Lakes Anthropology*. Edited by Eldon Johnson. St. Paul: Minnesota Historical Society.

Weeden, William B. (1890) *Economic and Social History of New England 1620–1789*. Boston: Houghton Mifflin.

Wijn, Jan Willem (1934) *Het krijgswezen in den tijd van Prins Maurits*. Utrecht: Drukkerij Hocijenbos & Co.

Wilkinson, Frederick (1971) *British and American Flintlocks*. (Country Life Collectors Guides Series). London: The Hamlyn Publishing Group Ltd.

———— (1970) *Guns*. London: Hamlyn Publishing Group Ltd.

Wilkinson, Henry (1973) *Engines of War.* Richmond, U.K: Richmond Pub. Co.

Williams, Roger (1934) *"Briefe Discourse on Warre,"* in *Memoir of Roger Williams, the Founder of the State of Rhode Island.* Reprint (original 1590). Edited by James D. Knowles. Boston: Lincoln, Edmonds and Co.

Winslow, Edward (1624) *Good News From New England.* London. I.D. for William Bladen and John Bellamie.

Winthrop, John (1972) *The History of New England From 1630–1649.* 2 vols. (First published in 1790 under title: *A journal of the transactions and occurrences in the settlement of Massachusetts and the other New England Colonies*). Reprint (of edition published in Boston by Phelps and Farnham in 1825 & 1826). Edited by James Savage. New York: Arno Press.

———— (1944) *Winthrop Papers.* Reprint (originals 1638–1644). Boston: Massachusetts Historical Society.

Winthrop, Robert C. (1867) *Life and Letters of John Winthrop 1630–1649.* Boston: Ticknor and Fields.

Wintringham, Tom (1943) *The Story of Weapons and Tactics: from Troy to Stalingrad.* Boston: Houghton Mifflin Co.

Wood, William (1865) *Wood's New England's Prospect, 1634.* Reprint. Boston: J. Wilson.

Woodward, Arthur (1960) "Some Notes on Gunflints," *Missouri Archaeologist.* 22:29–40.

Wray, Charles F. (1985) "Firearms Among the Seneca: the Archaeological Evidence," in *Proceedings of the 1984 Trade Gun Conference* (No. 18,2). Rochester: Rochester Museum of Science Center, 106–07.

Young, Alexander (1841) *Chronicles of the Pilgrim Fathers of The Colony of Plymouth From 1602 to 1625.* Reprint. 2nd ed. Boston: Charles C. Little and James Brown.